As Fred states in the introc .... qualified, compassionate, capable leaders now more than ever. Thank you, Fred, for shining the spotlight on the gold standard—Jesus was the original servant leader. Thanks also for taking Christ's countercultural message around the world... "Not so with you!"

Mark Miller
V.P. High Performance Leadership, Chick-fil-A, Inc.
International Best Selling Author of The Heart of Leadership

My good friend Fred Campbell has given us a biblically sound understanding of servant leadership. He presents this most critical topic in a provocative and insightful manner that will both inspire and challenge all of us to pursue and relate our Lord's definition of servant leadership to a contemporary culture that is in desperate need of spiritual guidance.

Dr. Tony Evans
President, The Urban Alternative
Senior Pastor, Oak Cliff Bible Fellowship

I have had the privilege of hearing Dr Campbell teach the material contained in this book to the leadership teams of two different churches with whom I have served in the UK. On each occasion we greatly benefited from the practical, biblical wisdom and principles taught, and from the experience of a man who clearly modelled them.

Given the many prominent abuses of leadership power we sadly read about every month, the clear call in this book to servant leadership could never be more relevant than it is today. The secular world is gradually catching on to the importance of this ancient leadership principle. I am convinced you will find this book an outstanding resource to help you become a more effective leader.

Phil Sweeting
Associate Pastor, Monyhull Church, Birmingham, England.

Henry Nouwen observed, "The beginning and the end of all Christian leadership is to give your life for others." Fred Campbell unpacks the breadth and nuances of authentic servant leadership better than anyone I know. His incisive new book, First Century Leadership for Twenty-First Century Christians, is drenched in biblical principles. I don't know of a more thorough, helpful book on servant leadership. Dr. Campbell has spent a lifetime studying and modeling Christ-honoring servant leadership. This book is on time and on target. Lift your life, humble your heart, and read this impactful book. You and everyone you influence will benefit.

David Shibley
Founder, Global Advance

Fred's Opus: Don't miss it! This book, *First Century Leadership for Twenty-First Century Christians*, summarizes Fred's life-long study and application of Servant Leadership. Don't miss it! This information has profoundly impacted the "Leadership Culture" of our entire ministry, which God has used to win more than 30 million people to Christ. Read on .... Don't miss it!

Andy Blakeslee
President, Here's Life Africa

Fred Campbell has been my pastor, mentor and friend since the day I first attended Faith Bible Church so many years ago and continues as he has ministered all over the world through Living Grace Ministries to bring the message of Servant Leadership to pastors, church leaders, missionaries, servants and, yes, to lay persons of which I am blessed to be one. As Fred has conveyed through his teaching, workshops, writings and correspondence, and which I now embrace, servant leadership applies to the secular world just as critically as in the outreach ministries. The next chapter in Fred's service is his book, *First Century Leadership for Twenty-First Century Christians*, which will lead the way in describing the biblical model of servant leadership for all of us.

Randall F. Adair
Attorney-at-Law

Wisdom is comprehensive insight into the ways and purposes of God. Wisdom is the right use of knowledge. Wisdom is the application of truth. My good friend Fred Campbell embodies these Christlike attributes and shares them with us in this practical and applicable expository of truth.

We have levels of leadership. We have seasons in our lives. Fred succinctly delivers these for our recognition and adoption. Obedience to the Word allows us to live and walk in the Wisdom, Will, and Way of God. Obedience allows us to go to a new level of living and a new level of leadership. The leadership modeled by the existential leader of all creation....our Lord and Savior Jesus Christ.

Fred reveals to us that Wisdom is more than just walking in its' path. Wisdom is also making a stand for moral rectitude and having the courage to endure, therefore modeling the true leadership of Christ.

Jesus said, "Your care for others is the measure of your greatness". (Luke 9:48b TLB) Our path to significance and true leadership is manifested in our care for others. So, let us embrace these divine principles and apply them to our lives and usher in the Kingdom of God on earth as it is in heaven.

Dr. John H. Binkley Jr.
Chairman Generational Group LLC, Dallas, TX

The call for leaders today is to lead like Jesus. In *First Century Servant Leadership for Twenty-First Century Christians*, Fred C. Campbell provides a timely, workable, and supportive toolkit for anyone aspiring to venture into the serious ministry to which our Lord Jesus has called the Church. He plainly describes how the twenty-first-century leaders that our people need are not leaders who serve to gain, but who serve to give; people who lead by serving others, empowering them to reach their full potential, and who are able to transform and integrate others. All Christians, and specifically those who fly the flag of leadership, will benefit hugely from reading these issues and implications of global leadership.

Bishop Dr Stanley Hotay
Director Here's Life Africa, Rooted in Jesus Tanzania
Bishop Anglican Diocese of Mt Kilimanjaro

First Century Leadership for Twenty-First Century Christians

First Century Leadership for Twenty-First Century Christians

FRED C. CAMPBELL

LIVING GRACE BOOKS

Dedication

I dedicate this book to my wife, Carolyn, who is the finest servant leader I know.

The book could not have been written without her support, love, and Christ-like example.

She is a woman of character and competent in the many things she does, giving all glory to her Savior and Lord. I'm sure that someday when she enters heaven, the Lord Himself will smile at her and say, "Well done, Carolyn, good and faithful servant."

Table of Contents

Author's Preface

Before His death, Jesus reminded His disciples of a secular leadership style in which leaders intimidate and dominate people. This model of leadership in Jesus' day was the corporate model—bossing, patronizing, commanding, controlling, and expecting gratitude for the slightest acts of kindness.

Jesus emphatically told the twelve, "It is not so among you" (Mark 10:43). Christ made sure His disciples understood they were to be servants who led for the benefit of others, not themselves. Their ambition was to make others successful, not to gain power for personal gain.

Effective leadership must be servant leadership, a radical concept for most of us. This form of leadership is intensely relevant for those serving as Christian leaders today.

This book is written primarily for Christian leaders who lead churches, local church ministries, organizations, mission agencies, and non-profits. However, the book has an application for leaders in the secular leadership field. That's why I added quotes from leaders and writers in the business arena, showing their agreement with biblical principles. Servant leadership is relevant to all leadership wherever influence occurs (families, education, schools, politics, athletics, etc.).

For the last 20+ years, it has been my joy and privilege to present the material in this book in 29 countries and 15 states. I do it in the form of a workshop combining teaching and small group discussions. Wherever I go, the need remains the same—effective Christian organizations need servants who lead well.

Servant leaders are leaders of character, men, and women who walk in integrity with skillful, competent hands motivated not by self-interest to get something but by self-sacrifice to give something—leaders who lead like the Lord Jesus.

Fred C. Campbell
Ovilla, Texas

Acknowledgements

I deeply appreciate those who have supported Living Grace Ministries over the years. You have served many around the world through this servant leadership ministry. Thank you for serving.

I want to thank Faith Bible Church of Desoto, Texas, and Grace Church, Ovilla, Texas, for allowing me to serve as their first senior pastor. We learned and loved together for God's matchless glory and by His amazing grace. He gets all the credit!

Also, my thanks and appreciation go to the members of the Living Grace Ministries Board of Directors. They were the ones who encouraged me to put the workshop material into a book. Thank you, Carolyn, Bob, David, Mark, and Andy.

My thanks to Wendy Stackable for her help in writing this book.

CHAPTER 1

Introduction and Overview

CHAPTER 1

Introduction and Overview

Since the beginning of time, people have looked for leaders to inspire and call them to action. Alexander the Great conquered the known world by the time he was 30 years old, but the Hellenistic kingdom splintered under the leadership of his generals.[1]

Peter the Great disguised himself as a worker to explore Western Europe, bringing its culture back home in the hope that he could modernize Russia; the result was a peasant revolt and changes that abandoned tradition in favor of progress.[2]

More recent leaders include Abraham Lincoln, Nelson Mandela, Mother Teresa, and Martin Luther King, Jr., all of whom significantly shaped culture.[3]

Researchers have tracked leadership shifts for more than 100 years, noting with difficulty the contradictions inherent in leadership models. More than 50 years ago, Warren Bennis observed:

Of all the hazy and confounding areas in social psychology, leadership theory undoubtedly contends for top nomination.... Probably more has been written and less is known about leadership than about any other topic in the behavioral sciences.[4]

Part of the problem stems from disputes regarding *nature* and *nurture*; in other words, are some people "born" leaders, or can anyone "learn" to lead?

At its core, most scholars believe that leadership is "an influencing process" that shapes followers and outcomes. Additionally, the leader's disposition and behavior create expectations and trigger responses.[5]

A BRIEF HISTORY OF LEADERSHIP STUDIES

Leadership theory emerged in the first part of the 20th century when intellectuals tried to explain why certain individuals motivate and inspire people while others try and fail.

Until about 1940, researchers believed that leaders were "exceptional individuals" who possessed "leadership traits," such as "intelligence and dominance."[6]

A decade later, theorists decided that leaders demonstrated leadership behavior, rather than personality strengths. In other words, leaders were task-oriented, supportive initiators.[71]

The research was inconsistent, though, so experts suggested that leaders emerged when conditions favored their appearance. Others hypothesized that certain individuals were leaders because they knew how to build relationships through mutual respect and trust. Other academics argued that leaders perform more impressively and their outcomes proved their leadership.[8]

In the 1980s, researchers decided that leaders *process information more quickly and accurately* than average people, setting them apart as individuals who can predict trends.[9]

Modern scholars claimed that real leadership is *transactional;* leaders comprehend what people want, and they know how to meet the need. Current thinking leans toward a belief that suggests that leaders know how to *transform people and situations* through vision casting, empathy, and charisma.[10]

Experts continue to debate the topic, but everyone agrees that we need qualified, compassionate, capable leaders now more than ever.

The 21st-century world is changing rapidly, presenting complex challenges that require wise, decisi By considering various examples of leadership, we see that biblical principles work best. The ultimate example is, of course, Jesus Christ, and we will spend most of our time discussing His leadership style.

DIFFERING VIEWS OF LEADERSHIP

For years, businesses, organizations, schools, churches, ministries, and policymakers have clung to a "leader-centric" paradigm, in which leaders hold power over their followers.[11]

Depending on the organization's mission, we tend to think about leadership from the perspective of these models:[12]

- **Democratic Leadership:** Everyone contributes to decisions.

- **Autocratic Leadership:** The person rarely consults with workers; the leader makes every decision of import.

- **Laissez-Faire Leadership:** The leader defers to workers, and decisions change according to preferences and productivity.

- **Strategic Leadership:** The leader strategizes with top managers, delegating responsibility according to skill sets.

- **Transformational Leadership:** The leader wants to advance the organization by pushing workers out of their comfort zones, encouraging them to innovate.

- **Transactional Leadership:** The leader incentivizes workers with rewards or punishments; the idea is to encourage workers to follow the "carrot" rather than earning the "stick."

- **Coach-Style Leadership:** The leader identifies strengths and weaknesses and helps workers develop a cumulative plan to grow as individuals and employees.

- **Bureaucratic Leadership:** While willing to listen to employees, the leader defaults to traditional methodologies if there is a conflict of interest.

The biblical model of leadership incorporates the best of the theories and models. In this book, we will explore transformational leadership in the context of scripture and through the lens of Servant Leadership.

Our position is that Servant Leaders welcome and initiate transformation whether in business, politics, education, ministry, or the family. Leaders must govern and lead people. While leaders may have impressive titles, such as CEO, lead pastor, board member, or headmaster, a leader's primary purpose should focus on serving.

Too many individuals step into a position of power, lacking biblical and practical training in leadership. They fall into leadership more by accident than design. As a result, some leaders are reluctant to take calculated risks because they do not want to embarrass themselves. Instead, they simply "wing it." Consequently, these insecure leaders often lose the opportunity to influence people and effect lasting change. In many instances, ineffective leaders adopt a hierarchical leadership style designed to control people, instead of fostering growth, trust, and creativity.

By contrast, Servant Leaders understand and competently fulfill their responsibilities of oversight. While power struggles may develop between the leader and his or her team members, a Servant Leader will resist the temptation to vie for a "throne of prominence." The effective Servant Leader values people over position, service over power, and vision over popularity.

SEVEN KEY COMPONENTS OF SERVANT LEADERSHIP

Some individuals have a natural tendency toward governance. However, managing people is not the same as leadership. Effective leaders do more than call people to action. They invite people to embrace their vision.

Genuine leadership garners loyalty, regardless of obstacles and setbacks. It inspires followers to strive for excellence. It motivates people to collaborate and innovate.

In one case, a leader with a magnetic personality may fail to attract and maintain the support that he or she needs. There can be numerous reasons for this disconnect, including a lack of focus or follow-through, inexperience, or poor communication skills.

In another case, a leader may equate leadership with control. However, history is replete with stories of powerful men and women who did not resort to manipulation or force to achieve their goals.

Conventional leadership models may rely on personality, opportunity, or outcomes, but Servant Leadership gazes past these peripherals toward eternity.

Seven distinctives characterize Servant Leaders.

1. Servant Leadership seeks good character above earthly praise.

Consider icebergs. The peaks of these "frozen mountains" often soar hundreds of feet above the surface of the water.[13] In 1987, scientists located an iceberg "roughly the size of the state of Rhode Island." Had it melted, the iceberg "could have supplied everyone in the world with 240 tons of pure drinking water."[14] Despite their formidable size, seven eighths of all icebergs remain *below* the waterline.[15]

That is a good picture of leadership. Most people focus on the visible part of the leader's "iceberg," including education, experience, communication skills, organizational ability, and willingness to resolve conflict. Indeed, most people trust the leader's charisma, competence, diligence, and networking skills. But that is only the tip; what lies beneath the surface?

We must look below the waterline to the individual's character. Servant Leadership *starts* with character. In other words, what is the leader like when they stand alone in the dark? Is the leader the same person in private as he or she is in public?

Although skill and experience count, a Servant Leader's character really determines effectiveness, driving decisions, and shaping actions.

Some people have impressive leadership aptitudes, but they have shoddy character. As a result, they often use their gifts to sway gullible followers.

In the context of Servant Leadership, leadership author and teacher Jim Rohn states that character refers to a personal commitment to integrity including honesty, loyalty, self-sacrifice, accountability, and self-control.[16] I would add to this list these qualities: wisdom, courage, discernment, perseverance, and justice.

2. A Servant Leader always considers the interests of the people that he or she leads.

A Servant Leader resolves to think of others first. This attitude is not only counter-cultural, it may seem counter-productive.

Typically, leaders focus on outcomes, including the bottom line or verifiable evidence of organizational growth. Traditional leaders typically define investments in terms of assets ("nickels and noses"), whereas the Servant Leader considers a wide range of investments, including the time and creative energy it takes to build and sustain a healthy organization. Frequently, these intangible investments emanate from workers, as well as managers, shareholders, or a church congregation.

Some leaders associate leadership with *fame*, so their goal is exposure. They promote themselves through books, seminars, television appearances, and social media. They reason, "If people know my name, they will remember my organization."

Of course, positive outcomes including financial stability, solidarity, and reputation, are important, but a Servant Leader will acknowledge that many people have invested their *lives* to help the organization or church succeed. These people must become a primary focus of the leader.

Ultimately, the leaders we truly admire are those who refuse to dominate the stage. They recognize and appreciate the contributions that other people have made. Rather than promoting themselves, they look for ways to encourage their constituents.

In other words, a Servant Leader makes room for *all* people, echoing Paul's words: "Do nothing out of selfish ambition or vain conceit. Rather, in humility value others above yourselves, not looking to your own interests but each of you to the interests of the others" (Philippians 2:3-4 NIV).

~ **DID YOU KNOW?** ~

James M. Kouzes and Barry Z. Posner co-authored a popular book about leadership called Credibility: How Leaders Gain It and Lose It, Why People Demand It, in which they describe formative stages of authentic leadership.[17]

One premise suggests that leaders who create an "environment of trust" empower their followers by giving them a voice. Consequently, employees actively participate in discussions about planning and growth strategies. According to Kouzes and Posner, these leaders foster a sense of belonging because they put other people ahead of themselves.[18]

3. A Servant Leader finds great satisfaction in the personal growth of people that he or she leads.

A Servant Leader is not simply a "boss." He or she is a "people developer." Instead of demanding, *Serve me, or else,* the Servant Leader asks, "How can I help *you* succeed?"

Corporate leader Max DePree states that the art of leadership is "liberating people to do what is required of them in the most effective and humane way possible." He believes that the best leader *removes obstacles* so followers can realize their potential.[19]

DePree wrote, "When we think about leaders and the variety of gifts people bring to corporations and institutions, we see that the art of leadership lies in polishing and liberating and enabling those gifts."[20]

The Servant Leader unleashes untapped potential, equipping *other* people to develop their own leadership skills.

4. A Servant Leader demonstrates love and compassion for the people that he or she leads.

By focusing on others, the Servant Leader can respond with empathy and kindness whenever there is a need. Too many leaders distance themselves from the people in the trenches, but a Servant Leader is not afraid to help shoulder the burden.

In many ways, a Servant Leader resembles the Good Samaritan in Jesus' famous parable from Luke chapter 10. The Samaritan saw the plight of a wounded man lying on the side of the road. Robbers had left him to die, and although other people had passed by, no one stopped to help. The Samaritan saw the need, felt compassion, and acted (Luke 10:25-37).

A Servant Leader recognizes the need and takes appropriate action, enlisting the aid of other capable individuals.

5. A Servant Leader listens.

Many leaders know how to communicate, but they fail to listen well. I suppose that many leaders expect people to listen to them since they have expertise and vision. They have the plan, means, and opportunity to succeed.

Yet, listening is crucial to success. It takes time and effort to develop consistent listening skills.

Servant Leaders practice active listening. In other words, they demonstrate comprehension and empathy. They can paraphrase what the other person said, then formulate questions that *establish* understanding.

According to one report, 70 percent of a leader's job includes listening, so it behooves the Servant Leader to develop solid listening skills.[21]

6. A Servant Leader demonstrates genuine humility.

Today, many people view humility as a weakness, particularly in the context of leadership. "Movers and shakers" are assertive, preemptive, and tenacious but Servant Leaders consider humility a strength.

Humility enables Servant Leaders to learn and adapt. According to entrepreneur Joe Ioracchi, humility is vital to Servant Leadership for several reasons.[22]

+ **Humility frees a person to acknowledge that there is something greater than oneself.**
+ **Humility connects leaders to their followers.**
+ **Humility inspires trust and respect.**
+ **Humility fosters sustainable excellence within the organization.**

In other words, Servant Leaders do not think less of themselves, as the adage goes, they just think about themselves less.

7. A Servant Leader is willing to share power with others as God directs.

Servant Leaders share power and responsibility because they know that their identity comes from the Lord Jesus, not their position or prestige. Servant Leaders benefit from the advice and help of other competent individuals. They see colleagues, co-workers, and subordinates as members of a team, all reaching for a common goal.

Servant Leaders do not need to horde power. Instead, they can invite other people to enter the conversation, so to speak. Market researcher James F. Hind sums up Servant Leadership this way:

Servant leadership combines a servant heart—softness, feeling, and generosity, with a corporate mind—tough-minded, realistic thought. Its keystone is concern for others—and communicating this attitude through actions that say, "I'm for you."[23]

Indeed, Servant Leaders establish an environment that allows people to thrive. Their people grow through respectful collaboration, resulting in instructive advice and a system of tangible and intangible rewards that inspire and motivate team members. The workers meet challenges with courage because they have *seen* authentic Servant Leaders share the load *and* share the victory.

Former president of Phoenix Seminary, Dr. Darryl DelHousaye wrote, "When people feel valued and trusted, supported, respected, advised, challenged, rewarded, inspired, motivated, and appreciated, they feel served, and when they feel served, they are experiencing the essence of servant leadership."[24]

Based on these insights, consider the following definition:

> *Servant Leadership is a leadership stance that submits to the authority of Jesus Christ, follows His example, and with integrity and humility, influences others for their benefit to accomplish the purposes of God in their lives.*

To put it another way, Servant Leadership is character and competency under the authority of Jesus Christ. We can look to King David's example:

> And David shepherded them with integrity of heart; with skillful hands he led them (Psalm 78:72 NIV).

David ruled with integrity *and* skill; indeed, David's integrity was foundational to his competency. There were no cracks in his leadership. It was sound and complete. If he made a promise, he kept it. If he began a job, he finished it. Though he was not sinless, he was blameless, being honest and open about his iniquity.

If a Christian leader is to function as an effective, biblical leader, he or she must emulate Jesus' leadership style, particularly since He is our greatest role model for life and work.

FIVE PRINCIPLES OF AUTHENTIC SERVANT LEADERSHIP

Servant Leadership hinges on five principles. Each concept builds on characteristics that I addressed in the preceding pages.

» Servant Leadership begins with a radical decision to reflect the attitude of Christ Jesus and to follow His example.

» Servant Leaders are committed to building and developing a unified team.

» Servant Leaders value healthy relationships.

» Servant Leaders have authority, but they use their power to serve, not to rule over others.

» Servant leadership is energized by humility.

Leaders have a "noble task," as the Apostle Paul tells the young pastor, Timothy (1 Timothy 3:1 NIV). God appointed leaders in the home, church, and society. Consider the way that Paul describes leadership in the Church:

> Although I hope to come to you soon, I am writing you these instructions so that, if I am delayed, you will know how people ought to conduct themselves in God's household, which is the church of the living God, the pillar and foundation of the truth (1 Timothy 3:14-15 NIV).

Notice the description here.

+ Paul says the Church is the "household of God." That means it is a warm, inviting, intimate setting. The people of God are family members.

+ The Church belongs to a living God, and He fills it with excitement and vitality.

+ The Church is also the pillar and foundation of truth, which means that its leaders must uphold and dispense truth faithfully and with wisdom.

~ WORTH QUOTING ~

J. Oswald Sanders wrote a classic book on spiritual leadership, asserting that leadership is indispensable to the individual and for society. "Ambition which centers on the glory of God and welfare of the church," he says, "is a mighty force for good."[25]

Additionally, we see the following traits of Servant Leadership when we study the lives of Peter and Paul:[26]

- Discipline, vision, wisdom, and the ability to make decisions
- Courage, humility, integrity, and sincerity
- A sense of humor, a righteous anger in the face of injustice, patience, friendship, and a willingness to tell the truth with tact
- The ability to inspire others, organizational skill, and the capacity to execute a plan
- The readiness to listen and write well
- Guidance and infilling by the Holy Spirit

Sanders concludes:
If the world is to hear the Church's voice today, leaders are needed who are authoritative, spiritual, and sacrificial. Authoritative, because people desire reliable leaders who know where they are going and are confident of getting there. Spiritual, because without a strong relationship to God, even the most attractive and competent person cannot lead people to God. Sacrificial, because this trait follows the model of Jesus, who gave Himself for the whole world and who calls us to follow in His steps.[27]

In the following chapters, we will look more closely at the life of Jesus, the ultimate Servant Leader, who reminded us of our mission as men and women of influence:

> "Instead, whoever wants to become great among you must be your servant, and whoever wants to be first must be your slave—just as the Son of Man did not come to be served, but to serve, and to give his life as a ransom for many" (Matthew 20:26-28 NIV).

According to leadership authors Warren Bennis and Burt Nanus, there are more than 350 definitions of leadership, but in their expert opinion, "leadership in its simplest form is the influencing of people."[28]

As a Christian leadership author, Hans Finzel agrees:

> Leadership is influence. Anyone who influences someone else to do something has led that person. Another definition might be, "A leader takes people where they would never go on their own."[29]

The best example of Servant Leadership, then, is Jesus Christ, who understands the connection between character and influence. He is the ultimate Servant, and He is the ultimate Leader.

THE LITMUS TEST OF CHARACTER

"Character" is who the leader is on the inside when no one else is around. Dr. Henry Cloud defines it as "the courage to meet the demands of reality."[30]

An effective leader, then, will set a good example through upstanding character. By emphasizing personal integrity, the leader can actually *expand* his or her influence.

Here is an overview that can inform your thinking about character as you read this book.

+ The Servant Leader is honorable; in other words, the Servant Leader demonstrates integrity, reliability, respect, and decency.

+ The Servant Leader respects a biblical code that values individuals for their unique abilities, experiences, and perspective.

+ The Servant Leader is willing to sacrifice self for the sake of others.

+ While the Servant Leader is competent and skilled, an authentic Servant Leader refuses to focus on self. Instead, the Servant Leader invests in others.

+ The Servant Leader is generous and consistently looks for active opportunities to bless people. The Servant Leader is not out to get anything, but to give, following the example of the Lord Jesus.

Ultimately, as Dr. Cloud puts it, a Servant Leader can inspire and influence people because he or she is a person of courageous character.

In the meantime, the world clamors for "superstar" leadership. We must resist the temptation to equate effectiveness with fame or outcomes. Instead, God is looking for leaders who give, rather than take, and who serve others, not themselves.

As *the* perfect Servant Leader, Jesus upholds this principle in various settings, with people from all walks of life, even in the face of betrayal and death. Therefore, it befits us to examine Servant Leadership through the lens of Christ's words, decisions, and actions.

The purpose of this book is to create an understanding of Servant Leadership and apply it to various settings. This is not a job description or outline that defines a person's function in an organization. Rather, this book asks the leader to examine heart, attitude, and habits so he or she can become an effectual Servant Leader in his or her leadership responsibility.

Chapter 1 Review
"Introduction and Overview"

- Differing Views of Leadership
  - » Democratic Leadership
  - » Autocratic Leadership
  - » Laissez-Faire Leadership
  - » Strategic Leadership
  - » Transformational Leadership
  - » Transactional Leadership
  - » Coach-Style Leadership
  - » Bureaucratic Leadership
- There are seven key components of Servant Leadership:
  - » A Servant Leader seeks good character above earthly praise.
  - » A Servant Leader always considers the interests of the people that he or she leads.
  - » A Servant Leader finds great satisfaction in the personal growth of people that he or she leads.
  - » A Servant Leader demonstrates love and compassion for the people that he or she leads.
  - » A Servant Leader listens.
  - » A Servant Leader demonstrates genuine humility.
  - » A Servant Leader is willing to share power with others as God directs.
- There are five principles of authentic Servant Leadership:
  - » Servant Leadership begins with a radical decision to reflect the attitude of Christ Jesus and to follow His example.
  - » Servant Leaders are committed to building and developing a unified team.
  - » Servant Leaders value healthy relationships.
  - » Servant Leaders have authority, but they use their power to serve, not to rule over others.
  - » Servant leadership is energized by humility.

Leadership is Risky Business

CHAPTER 2

Leadership is Risky Business

Although many people aspire to leadership, they often fail to recognize the inherent risks that accompany leadership. Let's go back to icebergs again. One in particular exposed the failed leadership of Mr. Edward John Smith.[31]

Captain Smith trained as a seaman and rose through the ranks, commanding various ships before receiving his last command as captain of the luxury liner, *Titanic*. The ship, famed even before its first voyage for its size and opulence, left Southampton to take on more passengers in France and Ireland. More than 2,200 souls set out for New York.[32]

After the first few days at sea, the crew received news that another ship, the *Caronia*, had seen ice in the path.[33] During the afternoon of the same day, Smith received a second warning, this time from the *Baltic*, about "dangerous ice."[34]

Ignoring the warnings, half an hour later, Smith attended a private party, at which he boasted to the dinner guests that if the ship were sliced into three sections, it would still float. In other words, the *Titanic* was virtually unsinkable.[35]

While Smith was at dinner, the crew received another warning from the *Californian*.[36] Then, around 11:40 p.m., a crew member spotted the iceberg. He reported the ship "scraped against the iceberg....Several holes have been made in the ship's side, allowing sea water to begin rushing in."[37]

Captain Smith rushed to the bridge to assess the damage, but the ship was already sinking. He ordered the crew to prepare lifeboats, but the ship was not equipped with enough rafts.[38] Captain Smith tried to manage the crisis, but 1,500 passengers, the captain, and the crew perished in the frigid waters of the North Atlantic. Only 713 people survived.[39]

Captain Smith's actions aboard the *Titanic* reflect a poor understanding of effective leadership and provide a perfect illustration of how poor leadership can devastate an organization. The *Titanic* was strong and solid, capable of crossing the sea with ease and comfort, but the great ship sank because its leader ignored warnings and misinterpreted facts.

Captain Smith's lack of leadership, especially in the face of crisis, resulted in devastation. Likewise, problems in today's organizations, schools, churches, and businesses can appear harmless at first but can, in fact, be "icebergs" that sink the ship.

Captain Smith's experience as a naval officer should have taught him to respond promptly and with discernment, but his experience alone was not enough. Effective leaders *develop* their leadership skills. They learn to listen well and communicate clearly. They work on problem solving, teamwork, and service. They seek successful mentors to help them grow. At the same time, they invest in the lives of their "crew."

Many leaders today still fail to see icebergs until it is too late. They may lack knowledge, understanding, or skills.

Becoming an effective leader requires time and effort. The first step is to identify unproductive tendencies and deal with them.

FIVE PROBLEMS WITH LEADERSHIP TODAY

Christian leader J. Oswald Sanders discovered that the term *leader* occurs only six times in the King James version of the Bible:

> That is not to say that the theme is not prominent in the Bible, but it is usually referred to in different terms, the most prominent being "servant." It is not "Moses, my leader," but "Moses, my servant." The emphasis is constant with Christ's teaching on the subject.[40]

Today, you can find scores of books that describe Christian leadership and many of them explore Servant Leadership. However, most authors address pastors and other ministry leaders, not men and women who occupy leadership positions in the secular arena. There is relatively little material available for lay leaders.

Hans Finzel, President of HDLeaders, believes that the average leader in a Christian setting faces at least five problems in learning to lead:[41]

- Today's leaders replicate the poor leadership habits of others.
- Today's leaders often lack basic skills for common leadership demands.
- Today's leaders lack good models and mentoring.
- Today's leaders lack formal training in leadership.
- Today's leaders are confused over the secular versus the spiritual in leadership.

Christian leaders, then, must learn to follow biblical guidelines and embrace fundamental concepts, applying them strategically within their organizations.

SERVANT LEADERSHIP IS ABOUT PEOPLE

At its core, leadership is *influence*. Leadership denotes neither rank nor status. Instead, it reflects an ability to identify and guide followers in a relationship with them.

~ WORTH QUOTING ~

Authors Larry Richards and Clyde Hoeldtke wrote:
To be named "servant" is to be recognized as one whom
God has shaped with special care and to whom He is
personally committed. To be named a servant by God is not
an inferior calling. God's servants are always special to Him....
Servanthood is a high and special calling that involves a
covenantal relationship with God. It is not a forced obedience
to a thoughtless master. There is instead a willing commitment
by the servant to a Master who fully commits Himself to the
servant as well.[42]

~ WORTH QUOTING ~

Phil Quigley, a former CEO, said, "I don't think of leadership
as a position or a skill. I think of leadership as a relationship."[43]
Researchers James M. Kouzes and Barry Z. Posner wrote:
Leadership is a reciprocal relationship between those who
choose to lead and those who decide to follow. Any discussion
of leadership must attend to the dynamics of this relationship.
Strategies, tactics, skills, and practices are empty unless we
understand the fundamental human aspirations that connect
leaders and their constituents.[44]

Corporate and civic leader Max DePree observed: Leadership
is an art, something to be learned over time, not simply by
reading books. Leadership is more tribal than scientific, more a
weaving of relationships than an amassing of information.[45]

Indeed, leadership is essentially a human investment. Dr. DelHousaye suggests:

> People are the greatest asset to any leader. Therefore, the ability to work with and through them is pivotal to effective leadership. Leadership is an investment into people which assists them in becoming successful for the good of the whole.[46]

Our culture does not always value servant leadership. We tend to want other people to serve *us*. We put our own concerns before others, rather than serving them and meeting *their* needs.

Christian management expert Myron Rush defines a servant as "one who meets the needs of the person he is serving."[47]

Theology Professor F. Duane Lindsey wrote about biblical servants:

> The word "servant" ranges in meaning from a slave to a vassal king but always refers to one characterized by dependence and servitude. Royal officials and personal representatives of a king were thus designated "servants." The term "servant" indicated a degree of honor, depending on the position of the one served. To be the "servant of God" denoted the highest honor.[48]

Robert Greenleaf, a senior corporate executive, declared that Servant Leadership is the *only* authority deserving one's allegiance. "Those who are committed to this principle," he wrote, "will respond to and follow only those leaders who demonstrate that they are servants."[49]

Greenleaf observed that Servant Leaders were also successful leaders because they understood the importance of service. He concluded: "The great leader is seen as servant first, and that simple fact is the key to his greatness."[50]

~ DID YOU KNOW? ~

In an article from Discipleship Journal, Francis Cosgrove summarized the following biblical qualities of a servant:[51]
- A servant is humble—He does not attract attention to himself (Matthew 10:24; 2 Timothy 2:25).
- A servant is diligent—He is actively working and not lazy (2 Timothy 4:2).
- A servant is busy serving—They are "busy about their business" of serving (2 Timothy 2:4).
- A servant should be able to teach—Mainly to teach other servants; not quarrelsome but kind (2 Timothy 2:24).
- A servant is patient—As opposed to resenting the circumstances in which he finds himself (2 Timothy 2:24).
- A servant is obedient—This is the "heart of servanthood" and the reason so many have problems with it (Ephesians 6:5-6; Titus 2:9).
- A servant is dedicated—He is totally committed to the one he serves (2 Samuel 5:12)
- A servant is watchful—He stays alerted and attentive to the needs his master may wish him to tend to (Luke 12: 35-36).
- A servant is faithful—He remains faithful to his master (1 Samuel 22:14).
- A servant does not talk back to his master—He respects his master (Titus 2:9).
- A Christian disciple-servant is Spirit-filled (Acts 2:16, 18).

SERVANT LEADERSHIP WORKS IN ALL SETTINGS

Servant Leadership is a style of leadership that soars above all the others, and the corporate world has recognized it effectiveness. For pragmatic reasons, many business and industry leaders recommend a form of Servant Leadership simply because it works.

For instance, C. William Pollard, Chairman Emeritus of The ServiceMaster Company, believes that "tomorrow's challenges require that its leaders be servant leaders."[52]

In searching for a model of leadership that is both inspirational and moral, academic researcher Jill Graham described a Servant Leader this way:

> It is the leader who models service by humbly serving the led, rather than expecting to be served by them. Therein is the paradox of servant-leadership. Leader-modeled service (or servant leadership) is a gift. It also tends to be contagious so that followers of servant leaders are inspired to pass on the gift.[53]

In other words, Servant Leaders are neither regulators nor controllers, but ministers. They inspire people to follow them because they model a combination of integrity, compassion, and respect.

Author James Means wrote:

> Servant leadership means that the leader best leads by serving. More than this, it means that one leads only by serving. Servant leadership is tested and authenticated by the measure of service rendered, not by effecting followers' compliance.[54]

~ WORTH QUOTING ~

Dr. Richard Love, a DMin graduate from Dallas Theological Seminary, wrote:
An effective Christian leader is a servant leader who maximizes his strengths, minimizes his limitations, and consistently grows in Christlike character in order to influence others in a way that helps them develop and accomplish a common vision.[55]

HEEDING THE CALL TO LEAD

When leaders fail, such as the captain of *Titanic*, followers suffer. In many ways, leaders resemble captains who guide a business, organization, school, church, ministry, or family over the seas of life. They set the course and determine the speed at which the "vessel" will travel. They motivate the crew, and they assume responsibility for the people on board.

Some people lead well, bringing their people safely to the destination; others fail miserably. When leaders disregard the seriousness of their call, they risk injuring their followers and, in many instances, they damage their own reputation as well.

I have served in leadership positions for over forty years, pastoring two churches and founding a ministry that trains Servant Leaders. During that time, I have come to two crucial conclusions:

First: Leadership is Not Optional

When I was a graduate student, I heard the late Dr. Howard Hendricks, a professor at Dallas Theological Seminary, say: "No church [or organization] can afford to hang a sign on its front door that says, 'No Help Wanted!'"[56]

Leadership is neither an option, nor a luxury; it is essential to the survival of the organization. Moreover, leadership impacts the entire community. *Everyone* either grows or regresses, depending on the leader's ability to listen and direct the people.

No business, organization, school, church, or ministry will succeed without good leadership. Even families flounder when husbands and wives abdicate their responsibilities.

In the absence of effective leadership come confusion and strife. Dreams fade, dedication wanes, enthusiasm dwindles, while criticism, cynicism, and frustration poison the atmosphere. Sooner or later, the whole mission grinds to a halt.

Second: The Essence of Good Leadership is Service.

Executive Robert Greenleaf surprised the corporate world with an illuminating description of leadership. The great leader, he posited, is a *servant* first and foremost.

But someone greater and smarter than Robert Greenleaf made this same observation over 2,000 years ago. Jesus chided His disciples as they jockeyed for position, saying:

> "You know that the rulers of the Gentiles lord it over them, and their high officials exercise authority over them. Not so with you. Instead, whoever wants to become great among you must be your servant, and whoever wants to be first must be your slave—just as the Son of Man did not come to be served, but to serve, and to give his life as a ransom for many" (Matthew 20:26 NIV).

The goal of leadership is not power. The goal is not fame or wealth. Effective leaders serve others and give their lives away as God directs. That is Servant Leadership.

Chapter 2 Review
"Leadership is Risky Business

- There are five problems with leadership today:
  - » Today's leaders replicate the poor leadership habits of others.
  - » Today's leaders often lack basic skills for common leadership demands.
  - » Today's leaders lack good models and mentoring.
  - » Today's leaders lack formal training in leadership.
  - » Today's leaders are confused over the secular versus the spiritual in leadership.
- We must define Servant Leadership in terms of influence.
- Servant Leadership works in all settings because the Servant Leader models integrity, compassion, and respect—qualities that businesses, organizations, schools, churches, and ministries need.
- We must heed God's call to lead others.
  - » Leadership is not optional.
  - » The essence of good leadership is service.

CHAPTER 3

Follow the Leader

Follow the Leader

A Servant Leader relinquishes whatever keeps him or her from serving others, promoting self-sacrifice.

A Servant Leader does menial tasks when necessary, promoting a renunciation of pride.

Servant Leadership is a journey that takes time. The route may seem circuitous and difficult. Nevertheless, each of us must embark on the journey if we hope to become authentic Servant Leaders with a journey that ends in heaven, where Jesus says, "Well done, good and faithful servant" (Matthew 25:19 NIV).

In the first chapter, we looked at the five principles of authentic Servant Leadership. Let's discuss them in greater detail now.

Servant Leadership begins with a radical decision to reflect the attitude of Christ Jesus and to follow His example.

First is a Christ-like attitude. A Servant Leader *thinks* like a servant. A Servant Leader *lives* like a servant. We have a godly example to follow. Servant Leaders think and live like the Lord Jesus, the ultimate Servant Leader.

Typically, we think of a servant as someone who is needy or disadvantaged, perhaps undereducated. Few people know the servant's name. A servant does not run a big company or command a big salary. At a banquet, the servant does not sit at the head table. The servant works behind the scenes, in the kitchen or cleaning up afterwards.

Few people would answer an ad that reads: "Servant wanted." Being a servant is not a dignified position, yet the gospels underscore Jesus' decision to serve. Jesus told His disciples, "...*for even the Son of Man* did not come to be served, but to serve, and to give his life as a ransom for many" (Matthew 20:28 and Mark 10:43 NIV).

Jesus came to serve. He did not seek fanfare. He sought neither riches, fame, nor popularity. He never angled for a position at the head table. Instead, He preferred to wash feet.

Jesus was a Servant who knew how to serve and give—and that is what Servant Leaders do best.

GIVING AS JESUS GIVES

The essence of all effective leadership is serving and giving.

We lead best when we serve. As theologian Henri J. M. Nouwen concluded: "A whole new type of leadership is asked for in the church of tomorrow, a leadership which is not modeled on the power games of the world, but on the servant-leader, Jesus, who came to give his life for the salvation of many."[57]

Consider this compelling description of Servant Leadership:

> Do nothing out of selfish ambition or vain conceit. Rather, in humility value others above yourselves, not looking to your own interests but each of you to the interests of the others. In your relationships with one another, have the same mindset as Christ Jesus: Who, being in very nature God, did not consider equality with God something to be used to his own advantage; rather, he made himself nothing by taking the very nature of a servant, being made in human likeness. And being found in appearance as a man, he humbled himself by becoming obedient to death—even death on a cross (Philippians 2:3-8 NIV).

This passage speaks of utter selflessness. This was the attitude that "launched [Jesus] from the splendor of heaven to a humble manger in Bethlehem," and later, to die on the cross at Calvary.[58]

Unselfishness cost Jesus His life, but it marked Him as a loving servant. The call to Servant Leadership means dying to yourself and rejecting the temptation to focus only on your needs, goals, and plans.

THE MIND OF CHRIST

Paul wrote that Servant Leadership begins in the mind. It reflects the attitude of Jesus Christ (Philippians 2). What does that mean? Consider the evidence:

- Jesus expressed the very nature of God; therefore, He was equal with God the Father, enjoying the benefits of deity.
- He co-existed with God the Father and God the Holy Spirit.
- He was not a created being.
- He was not inferior to God. He was not God's assistant, doing the things that God the Father did not want to do. He was not second in command or next in line for the throne of heaven.

In heaven, Jesus enjoyed all the benefits of divinity. All of creation worshiped Him. He was the wise and benevolent Creator. He had neither limitations nor restrictions. He never had to get permission to act. He was omniscient, omnipresent, and omnipotent. He lived in a perfect environment, enjoying perfect fellowship with God the Father and God the Holy Spirit.

Theologian Gordon Fee explains that Jesus entered human history "not as Lord, but as a slave, a person without advantages, with no rights or privileges, but in servanthood to all."[59] The infinite God became incarnate, and the incarnate Man became a slave, obedient to death.

Jesus loved us, so He "made himself nothing by taking the very nature of a servant, being made in human likeness" (Philippians 2:7 NIV).

Although Jesus is fully human, He is also fully divine. By contrast, you are simply human.

Everything about you is human. You think like a human, you experience human emotions, and you make human choices. Everything about you mirrors your humanity. By contrast, Jesus is fully God and fully human.

Jesus made a radical decision to become "nothing." He emptied Himself without giving up His deity. He walked away from His personal privileges to become a man. He left perfect heaven to live on imperfect earth.

Jesus was born to commoners in a small-town barn. When He began His public ministry, people questioned His motives. In the end, men spit on Him, tortured Him, then nailed Him to a cross. He gave up *everything* to secure our salvation and to give us peace with God the Father. Although Jesus is the King, worthy of our worship, He viewed humility as a necessity.

His mindset is to be our mindset. Let's say that I have extra money in my bank account. I could use the money to buy something for myself, such as a new house or a car. I could buy something that brings me pleasure or meets a need. I could put the money in a bank, where it might earn interest. I could invest the money. In each case, the money benefits *me*. Or, if I notice someone else has a problem, I could renounce my own pleasure or comfort for the sake of the other person and give them the money.

That is what Jesus did. He knew that we could never escape the grip of sin without His help. He sacrificed Himself to set us free and to give us eternal life. Jesus made that choice.

Jesus took the form of a "bond-servant" (Philippians 2:7 NASB). According to scholars, the term comes from the Greek word *doulos*, which refers to a person who was obligated to serve others.[60]

As a man, Jesus chose to become a servant, and by doing so, He revealed God's character and purpose for humanity.

Jesus consistently demonstrated love, power, and wisdom through His service to others. He ministered to lepers and beggars. He forgave prostitutes and tax collectors, and He gave hope to people who lived on the "fringes" of society, like the Samaritan woman at the well. He held nothing back.

Servant Leaders adopt Christ's grace-filled attitude to seek the welfare of others.

THINKING AS JESUS THINKS

When we refer to "thinking the way that Jesus thinks," we must remember that Jesus gave up everything to serve people. He thinks about people from all walks of life, with diverse experiences, personalities, and gifts. He thinks about their potential, their needs, and their goals. Most importantly, He thinks about the Father's plan for their lives.

As we learn to think as Jesus thinks, we develop a *radical commitment* to love, creating opportunities to serve and lead in a way that transforms people and communities.

LIVING AS JESUS LIVED

Servant Leaders reflect the mind of the Lord Jesus and follow His example.

John described Jesus' last Passover meal with His disciples. As they walked into the Upper Room, they took their seats. Normally, the servant would kneel with a basin of water, removing the guests' sandals, then carefully clean the dust or mud from the weary guests' feet.[61] On this occasion, though, no one cleaned the disciples' feet. And, none of Jesus' followers volunteered to wash the feet of their friends, or even His feet.

As Jesus walked to the table, perhaps He thought about His many teachings on servanthood. Perhaps He thought about the examples He had set for His disciples. Had His followers listened and learned? He was clearly the leader, yet he humbled Himself before His men. During the meal, when no one made a move to wash feet, Jesus made His move (John 13:1-17). In that moment, we see several principles of Servant Leadership.

LEADING AS JESUS LEADS

1. Servant Leaders do not draw attention to themselves.

Jesus slipped away from the table. He pulled off His outer robe, wrapped the towel around His waist, then poured water into a bowl. He went to His disciples and washed their dirty feet.

He did not draw attention to Himself. He didn't say, "Hey guys, watch Me serve you. This is good stuff. John, when you write this chapter, mark it with red letters." He simply stooped to serve. He did not put the foot washing on Instagram. He did not send anyone a text or video about the event.

From Jesus' example, we learn that Servant Leaders initiate affirming actions that benefit others without drawing attention to themselves. Jesus did not call a committee meeting to discuss the merits of foot-washing. He gave them an example to imitate and practice among themselves.

Servant Leaders do not serve in absentia or at arm's length. Indeed, Servant Leadership will require you to submit yourself to others, doing the menial tasks that no one else wants to do.

Nothing is ever beneath the dignity of a Servant Leader. When you understand this principle, you will begin to understand the importance of living as Jesus lived.

At times, Servant Leaders clean toilets if necessary and take meals to senior citizens. They visit patients in the hospital when possible. They comfort the lonely. They set aside their busyness to help others. They do not seek to be noticed or expect anything in return. They simply want to serve and give.

2. Servant Leaders offer to help, despite difficult circumstances.

Peter did not want Jesus to wash his feet. He thought this act of service was beneath his Lord. Similarly, some people feel awkward when a leader offers to serve them.

I remember reaching out to an elderly woman in one of my churches. I wanted to check on her and offered to schedule a short visit, but when I called, she said, "What do you want?" She felt uncomfortable with the idea of my visit and opted out.

Jesus confronted Peter's resistance with truth, patience, and love. "Unless I wash you, you have no part with Me," Jesus told Peter (John 13:8 NIV).

Servant Leaders may face opposition. When they do, they continue to serve in the best way they can. They demonstrate respect, empathy, benevolence, and humility.

Remember, Jesus even washed the feet of *Judas*. Although Jesus knew He was about to die, and He knew Judas had already decided to betray Him, the Master knelt before Judas and washed His errant disciple's dusty feet.

The Servant Leader looks for ways to serve others, even if it seems awkward or challenging. Be persistent and patient. Love *intentionally.*

3. Servant Leaders see the need and get involved.

After washing the disciples' feet, Jesus used the moment to teach His followers a valuable lesson:

> "Do you understand what I have done for you? . . . You call me 'Teacher' and 'Lord,' and rightly so, for that is what I am. Now that I, your Lord and Teacher, have washed your feet, you also should wash one another's feet. I have set you an example that you should do as I have done for you" (John 13:12-15 NIV).

When someone is sinking, the Servant Leader will throw the person a rope. Whether a person needs prayer, correction, or advice, the Servant Leader notices. Sometimes the Servant Leader enlists the help of other qualified individuals who know *how* to help. The bottom line is, the Servant Leader sees the need and consistently shares the love of Jesus.

4. Servant Leaders do not seek status.

In case you wondered, there is no "Hall of Fame for Servant Leaders."

In fact, Servant Leaders rarely command impressive salaries, and few luminaries ever applaud them for their efforts.

Yet, whenever a true Servant Leader stands before the Lord Jesus, he or she will hear these words: "Well done, thou good and faithful servant" (Matthew 25:21).

Servant Leadership reflects the greatness of Christ. That is why the commitment to Servant Leadership requires a *radical decision.*

An unmarried missionary named Angie Garber worked with Native American Navajos for many years. She lived in a small house with few comforts. From the world's perspective, Angie was a "nobody," yet according to her obituary, Angie was a shining star:

> It took Garber a little time at first to appreciate where God had called her. She said, "When I first came here to serve, I thought this was the most desolate place in the world. I called it a desert." She eventually came to view the reservation as an oasis. Every day, Garber ministered to and befriended people who are easily misunderstood because of cultural differences....
>
> "The issue is not how many people come to know the Lord or not; the main thing is: Is your heart for the Lord? If you didn't love the Lord, you couldn't work or serve here," explained Garber. For her, love was everything. It had to be unconditional, and it often came from sharing life with the people around her.
>
> Being a servant offers no guarantees that love will be returned. Garber said, "The only heart that can love is one that is broken. You wouldn't have much love if you couldn't share the heartaches." In ministry, she had her fair share of broken hearts, but her choice to love brought blessings as well. "If you love somebody, then you are going to be a blessing to them. You don't even feel like you are being a servant to someone, if you love them." [62]

If you hope to be a Servant Leader, you must give as Jesus gives, think as Jesus thinks, live as Jesus lives, and lead as Jesus leads. In short, if you hope to become a Servant Leader, you must serve as Jesus serves.

Chapter 3 Review
"Follow the Leader"

- Servant Leadership begins with a radical decision to reflect the attitude of Christ Jesus and to follow His example.

- Servant Leaders live like Jesus, with compassion and love.

- Servant Leaders give as Jesus gives, with generosity and selflessness.

- Servant Leaders seek to have the mind of Christ:

  » They embrace humility and grace.

  » They are willing to serve, even when the work seems "beneath" them.

  » They recognize their limitations and rely on Jesus for discernment and guidance.

- Servant Leaders think like Jesus:

  » Jesus thinks about people from all walks of life, with diverse experiences, personalities, and gifts.

  » Jesus thinks about people's potential and the Father's plan for their lives.

- Servant Leaders follow Jesus' example by serving with humility.

- Servant Leaders lead as Jesus leads:

  » They do not draw attention to themselves.

  » They help people, despite the circumstances.

  » They see the need and get involved.

  » They avoid the temptation to seek status.

CHAPTER 4

The Team with Purpose

The Team with Purpose

A Servant Leader builds, develops, and leads a team that loves each other, promoting team oneness.

Learning to be an effective Servant Leader is a journey that requires *intentional* steps toward change. First, you must reflect the mind and the attitude of the Lord Jesus and follow His example of service and leadership. Second, you must develop a solid team.

Servant Leaders commit themselves to building and developing a unified team.

Humble Servant Leaders understand that healthy teamwork brings success. Great accomplishments occur because faithful, inspired people collaborated. They pooled their ideas and resources, working toward a common objective.

You must accept that your business, organization, school, church, ministry, political group, or family cannot revolve around you. You *need* the team, and together the team can do more, with better results.

Suppose there is a massive table in the middle of my living room. Due to its size, the table is heavy. If I want to move it to the dining room, I could either inch the table to its new location, or I could ask a few friends to help carry the table together.

Servant Leadership focuses on the team, acknowledging that we are better when we are together.

~ **WORTH QUOTING** ~

As Benjamin Franklin was signing the Declaration of Independence, he famously quipped, "We must all hang together, or assuredly we shall all hang separately."[63]

Ironically, some of life's most inspiring quips appear on t-shirts. You might call it "truth on a tee." I saw a t-shirt that pictured a group of friends clinging to a rope as they scaled a mountain. On the front, the t-shirt declared: "TEAM." On the back, the t-shirt simply said, "24 guys hanging on the same rope."

Working toward a common goal invigorates team members and inspires them to persist, despite setbacks or impending trouble. Whenever a leader considers himself or herself a "maverick" or "Lone Ranger," problems follow, including missed deadlines, diminished returns, or mission drift.

By contrast, a team can accomplish great things when they work together for a common goal. For instance, my favorite baseball team hailed from Pleasantville, a small town in New Jersey—the Greyhounds. I played third base my senior year. We dominated our high school league. With two exceptions, no other team outplayed us. We outpitched, outran, and outcoached the opposition. Our success flowed from a commitment to teamwork. We were not a group of individuals; we were a unit. We achieved our goal by following two rules:

• "Remember that you are a team on the field."

• "Remember that you are a team off the field."

We sat together in class, we studied together, we ate lunch together, and we left the locker room for practice as a team. We even had our own song. Everything we did reflected our loyalty and responsibility to the team.

SERVANT LEADERS CAST A CLEAR VISION

Sometimes a team will follow anyone who barks loudly enough or who sounds authoritative; however, a successful team will only continue to follow a leader who demonstrates integrity, wisdom, and empathy.

Servant Leaders do not simply "rally the troops." They cast a vision that inspires hope, creativity, and confidence.

Servant Leaders cast the vision, describe the need for action, and explain guiding principles. For instance, if you are a pastor, you might dream of planting churches around the world. Or, maybe you are a coach who wants your players to implement a new training regimen. Or, perhaps you are the president of a company, and you plan to roll out an innovative product or service. Regardless, your vision will almost certainly stall unless you build a cohesive team that embraces your vision, loves each other, and knows how to execute a plan.

GOD BELIEVES IN TEAMWORK

We must remember that God believes in teamwork. The Holy Trinity is a team, comprised of God the Father, God the Son, and God the Holy Spirit (Matthew 28:19). The Bible records numerous examples of effective teamwork.

- In Exodus chapter 18, Moses felt overwhelmed listening to the people's troubles. He was utterly exhausted. His father-in-law, Jethro, suggested that Moses delegate some of the responsibility, thus dividing the labor. As a result, Moses created a team to help him attend to the people's needs.

- God directed Gideon to select 300 warriors to fight the Midianites. Together, they defeated a fierce army (Judges 7).

- David's mighty men repeatedly followed their king into battle. David's "team" preserved the throne despite overwhelming odds (2 Samuel 23:8-39).

In Ecclesiastes, we read:

Two are better than one, because they have a good return for their labor: If either of them falls down, one can help the other up. But pity anyone who falls and has no one to help them up (Ecclesiastes 4:9-10 NIV).

The New Testament also describes the effectiveness of teamwork:

- Jesus never ministered alone. In the beginning, Jesus had a small team of four followers who followed Him (Matthew 4:18-22). Eventually, He called twelve disciples who became apostles, and they spent three years watching and learning from their Master (Matthew 10:1-4). Even after Judas died, the apostles replaced him with a team member who would join them in Christ's glorious mission (Acts 1:12-23).

- After Jesus returned to heaven, the Holy Spirit filled Christians in Jerusalem. No single individual exerted control over the early Church. Leaders emerged to direct local churches and commission missionaries. A council of elders decided that Gentiles could embrace the Gospel like the Jews (Acts 15).

- The Antioch Church sent missionary *teams* to proclaim the Good News, starting with Paul and Barnabas, then Paul and Silas, and finally, Barnabas and John Mark (Acts 13-18).

- Paul appointed leadership *teams* of deacons who attended to daily or weekly needs, such as caring for widows. In addition, teams of pastors, evangelists, and teachers preached and taught the people (Acts 6; Philippians 1; 1 Timothy 3).

In short, the first-century Church valued teamwork, and they authorized groups of godly men and women to fulfill the Great Commission of our Lord Jesus Christ.

SERVANT LEADERS KNOW THAT EVERY PERSON ON THE TEAM MATTERS

Sometimes, a Servant Leader may function like an athletic coach.

Imagine that you are directing a soccer team. You know that everyone on the team has a specific role to play, so you evaluate a player's skills and assign the person to a position on the field. You expect your team members to pass the ball, moving it down the field toward the goal. You realize that the best player will not score goals all the time. In fact, the only way to win is through effective teamwork. Whenever a player drives the ball into the net, the entire team celebrates.

Some team members are more visible than others. They have "important" jobs, like managing a department or overseeing a project. By contrast, other team members work quietly behind the scenes, verifying details or balancing ledgers. Regardless, every team member matters. Wise Servant Leaders will learn to appreciate—and validate—the entire team.

TEN CHARACTERISTICS OF A HEALTHY TEAM

Servant Leaders know how to build solid teams and create a safe environment that fosters respect and trust. Moreover, they identify potential snags while promoting healthy collaboration.

1. A unified team shares a sense of purpose and vision.

Notice the key words here: purpose and vision.

Purpose points to calling. In other words, why does your business, organization, school, church, ministry, or political group exist? Consider these questions regarding purpose:

+ Why did God bring your group together?
+ Why did you move your organization to its current location?
+ What do you believe your organization can achieve?

Vision refers to a clear and compelling picture of the future, producing passion, loyalty, and growth. Consider these questions related to vision:

+ What do you hope to accomplish over the next five years?
+ What "impossible dream" has God laid on the heart of your leadership team, and how might that dream shape the organization?
+ How does your organization's vision reflect the team's passion? What are you doing to inspire loyalty and growth?

Remember, an organization's vision must be consistent and exhibit purpose. Vision, then, gives the people a sense of direction.

Vision keeps the team heading in the same direction. Team members become like arrows flying toward a bullseye that you identified in your mission statement.

2. Members of an effective team enjoy each other.

The most productive and successful teams prioritize relationships. As a result, the atmosphere is relaxed and comfortable. There is a lack of tension and boredom. Instead, team members are focused and motivated. They take pride in their work. Employees avoid gossip and backbiting because they realize that negative behavior erodes morale and damages everyone in the organization.

In the Gospels, we read that "Jesus went up on a mountainside and called to him those he wanted, and they came to him" (Mark 3:13 NIV). Jesus wanted to be with and relate to His team.

~ DID YOU KNOW? ~

In a safe setting, co-workers build trust as they labor together toward a common objective. Here are a few features of a healthy office:

- Colleagues laugh together at work. They view each other as associates, not competitors.
- The team exudes energy. Servant Leaders encourage team members to share ideas, creating interest in the organization's welfare.
- Team members practice active listening when others are speaking. Individuals feel safe, knowing that peers and administrators listen to them.
- The team members spend time with each other outside of work, building healthy relationships that foster camaraderie.

An effective Servant Leader will provide an environment that invites people to cooperate, grow, and innovate. Servant Leaders offer recurring opportunities for the team to get to know each other. A healthy team can help the leader achieve the vision that God has placed on his or her heart.

3. A flourishing team practices "HOT" communication.

Paul reminds Christians that Jesus gave the Church various leaders to provide oversight, and when there is a problem, the team should speak the truth with love:

> Let your conversation be always full of grace, seasoned with salt, so that you may know how to answer everyone (Colossians 4:6 NIV).

He expands our responsibility to include guarding our words:

> Do not let any unwholesome talk come out of your mouths, but only what is helpful for building others up according to their needs, that it may benefit those who listen (Ephesians 4:29 NIV).

Servant Leaders encourage "HOT" communication, applying the following biblical principles:

- **H for HONESTY.** Set a good example that team members want to follow. Do not lie or manipulate the facts to suit your desires.

- **O for OPENNESS.** Urge your team members to speak freely, without the fear of criticism or mockery. No one in your organization should feel embarrassed to make suggestions.

- **T for TRANSPARENCY.** Encourage team members to embrace authenticity. No one should feel the need to "fake it" or "perform" to gain approval, including you.

Since HOT communication is honest, open, and transparent, your team members will feel empowered to challenge, correct, advise, and support each other with grace and love.

~ DID YOU KNOW? ~

According to Harvard communication experts, Ralph G. Nichols and Leonard A. Stevens, active listening includes four stages:[64]

- Listening to the speaker and anticipating where the conversation will go, then trying to draw conclusions to further the discourse
- Weighing the speaker's evidence, determining whether it is valid or complete
- Summarizing the speaker's comments, mentally noting key points
- Listening beneath the surface and reading facial expressions and body language, searching for meaning through non-verbal cues

4. A great team practices active listening.

Anyone can hear a person speak, but it takes time and effort to listen. Active listening gives the speaker the attention that he or she deserves, then demonstrates comprehension and understanding. For instance, the listener should be able to paraphrase the high points of the speaker's conversation and respond appropriately.

You must practice active listening and teach your followers to do the same. Doing so can establish an atmosphere of trust and unity on your team.

Active listening can be exhausting. It requires commitment. Many leaders wrongly assume that listening is a passive activity, but nothing could be further from the truth. On average, people hear "between 20,000 and 30,000 words during the course of a 24-hour period."[65] Think about that. Every day, people are trying to process over 20,000 words, sorting through data, trying to make sense of it all.

People encounter huge waves of information, but for the most part, they retain only a small portion. But active listening differs from this coincidental experience of hearing people speak.

~ DID YOU KNOW? ~

In 2020, Forbes reported a study that described the connection between listening and retention. Here are their exact findings:[66]

- 85 percent of what we know we have learned through listening.
- Humans generally listen at a 25 percent comprehension rate.
- In a typical business day, we spend 45 percent of our time listening, 30 percent of our time talking, 16 percent reading and 9 percent writing.
- Less than 2 percent of all professionals have had formal education on learning to understand and improve listening skills and techniques.

5. A successful team values the contributions that every person makes.

No one on the team is more important than the others. Although roles may differ, each person contributes to the organization's growth and wellbeing.

The Chicago Bulls provided an excellent example when they won six NBA championships because they put the team before the stars and coaches.[67] They learned to work through their conflicts and take the court as a unit. They respected each other. They understood their strengths and weaknesses. They supported each other through injuries and mishaps.

The human body provides an excellent example as well. Paul said that each part of the body needs the other parts to function correctly:

> Just as a body, though one, has many parts, but all its many parts form one body, so it is with Christ. For we were all baptized by one Spirit so as to form one body—whether Jews or Gentiles, slave or free—and we were all given the one Spirit to drink. Even so the body is not made up of one part but of many.
>
> Now if the foot should say, "Because I am not a hand, I do not belong to the body," it would not for that reason stop being part of the body. And if the ear should say, "Because I am not an eye, I do not belong to the body," it would not for that reason stop being part of the body.
>
> If the whole body were an eye, where would the sense of hearing be? If the whole body were an ear, where would the sense of smell be? But in fact God has placed the parts in the body, every one of them, just as he wanted them to be. If they were all one part, where would the body be?
>
> As it is, there are many parts, but one body. The eye cannot say to the hand, "I don't need you!" And the head cannot say to the feet, "I don't need you!" On the contrary, those parts of the body that seem to be weaker are indispensable, and the parts that we think are less honorable we treat with special honor. And the parts that are unpresentable are treated with special modesty, while our presentable parts need no special treatment. But God has put the body together, giving greater honor to the parts that lacked it, so that there should be no division in the body, but that its parts should have equal concern for each other (1 Corinthians 12:12-25 NIV).

In His great wisdom, God created people to thrive in community, working and serving alongside one another, like a championship team or a healthy body.

6. An effective team acknowledges the importance of a primary leader.

While everyone on the team fulfills a unique role, primary leaders should guide the team with wisdom and kindness. Sometimes, the Servant Leader calls for action. At other times, the Servant Leader must assume responsibility for missteps or deflect unwarranted criticism.

You will undoubtedly grow into your position. The team can help you evolve by showing support and loyalty while also giving you honest feedback.

Throughout Scripture, God commissions fallible men and women to lead others in a primary role. For example:

- Moses led the people out of Egyptian bondage.
- God directed Moses to part the Red Sea, then lead the children of Israel through the desert for forty years. During that time, Moses taught the people about God's character, His Law, and His purpose for their lives (Exodus 14-Deuteronomy 34).
- God appointed Joshua to lead the Israelites into the Promised Land, where they conquered mighty nations, finally possessing the Promised Land (Joshua 1-24).
- God empowered Deborah to lead the Israeli army to victory against the fierce Midianites (Judges 4).
- God enabled David to establish the kingdom of Israel, authorizing him to rule with justice, despite uprisings and David's personal failures (1 Samuel 16-1 Kings 2).
- God galvanized Peter so that he preached to thousands, despite his tendency toward impulsiveness and fear. Later, an emboldened Peter helped lead the Church during a time of intense persecution (Acts 2-6; 1 Peter 1-5; 2 Peter 1-3).

- God called Lydia, who became the first Christian convert in Europe, to use her influence to advance the gospel (Acts 16:11-15).

- God inspired Jesus' brother, James, to guide the Church in Jerusalem, despite increasing persecution (Matthew 13:55; Mark 6:3; 1 Corinthians 15:7; Galatians 1:18-19; Acts 12:1-17; James 1-5).

And as we saw earlier, God commissioned Paul, Barnabas, Silas, and John Mark to launch churches around the ancient world. These faithful men led their teams through exciting and dangerous times. Whether or not they felt qualified, they responded to God's invitation to lead and serve.

A great example of primary leadership is Titus. Paul encouraged Titus to pick up the mantle. As a leader, Titus appointed new leaders and a group of elders, who continued to advance the gospel in surrounding cities:

> To Titus, my true son in our common faith: Grace and peace from God the Father and Christ Jesus our Savior. The reason I left you in Crete was that you might put in order what was left unfinished and appoint elders in every town, as I directed you (Titus 1:4-5).

Paul recognized Titus' skills and potential, so he entrusted Titus with special authority as a primary leader.

7. A strong team can weather disagreement and tension.

Servant Leaders realize that every organization must deal with conflict sooner or later. Rather than running from it or blaming someone, effective leaders look for healthy solutions.

Sometimes, leaders view struggling team members as liabilities, but a Servant Leader seeks to mentor them in their struggle. A Servant Leader will identify the source of trouble and find constructive ways to address the issue.

You must not allow disagreements to devolve into division. Often, disagreements stem from differences of opinion, but opposing views do not have to lead to squabbles. As a Servant Leader, you should encourage gracious and frank discussion, consistent cooperation, and agree to disagree when necessary.

8. A dynamic team shares the work for the sake of shared glory.

Unity tends to promote celebration, whereas discord produces suspicion, jealousy, gossip, and resentment. When everyone commits to a common vision, the team can operate efficiently. People begin to collaborate and innovate. Everyone shares the glory when everyone shares the work.

Personal success accentuates team success. Your team members may boast, "Hey! Look what *I* did!" Encourage them to say and affirm, "Look at what *we* accomplished!"

9. A healthy team affirms the strengths of its members, while helping weaker members improve.

Peter Drucker said, "The task of leadership is to create an alignment of strengths so strong that it makes the system's weaknesses irrelevant."[68]

Affirm team members who exude strength. Help team members who are struggling. Step in to correct or redirect the individual. Your goal is the health of the organization and the health of the team.

10. Effectual teams "do life" together.

A strong team functions like a community where the people know each other deeply, serve one another willingly, and care for one another genuinely. Encourage oneness and fellowship so your team members see themselves as integral parts of a community. This honors each individual's gifts, time, and contributions.

As a Servant Leader, remember that your team members have families to consider and obligations outside of work. Set and respect boundaries.

SERVANT LEADERS DEVELOP THE TEAM

Servant Leaders can follow these concise principles for developing a community of life:

+ Demonstrate grace as you share the vision.

- Trust and value each member of your team.
- Communicate clearly and express gratitude.
- Practice active listening while affirming individuals on your team.
- Respect each person's contribution and look for ways to serve the team.
- Encourage the team to follow you; set a good example.
- Face conflict honestly; demonstrate love.
- Build a community by sharing the work *and* the glory.
- Affirm your team's strengths, then address the weaknesses with grace.
- "Do life" together.

Teamwork is not easy, and there will be obstacles. Some people on the team may resist change. As a Servant Leader, gently redirect them so that they can thrive.

Explain your vision clearly and give your team members *time* to embrace change. Sometimes, a team member has a competing vision. If that happens, you must clarify instructions so that everyone is working toward a common goal.

As a Servant Leader, train your people. At times, you will need to disciple team members yourself. At other times, you can appoint a qualified mentor to answer questions and guide the team.

At the core of every thriving organization, there is a unified leadership team that loves each other.

A healthy team looks like the picture on that t-shirt: "24 guys hanging together on the same rope."

Chapter 4 Review
"The Team with Purpose"

+ Servant Leaders cast a clear vision.

+ God believes in teamwork.

+ Servant Leaders know that every person matters.

+ Ten characteristics of a healthy team:

  » A unified team shares purpose and vision.

  » Members of an effective team enjoy each other.

  » A flourishing team practices HOT communication.

    ◊ H stands for HONESTY

    ◊ O stands for OPENNESS

    ◊ T stands for TRANSPARENCY

+ A great team practices active listening.

+ A successful team values the contributions that every person makes.

+ An effective team acknowledges the importance of a primary leader.

+ A strong team weathers disagreements and tension.

+ A dynamic team shares the work for shared glory.

+ A healthy team affirms the strengths of its members, while helping weaker members improve.

+ Members of an effective team "do life" together.

  » Servant Leaders develop the team.

"The single most important distinctive of effective teams from ineffective teams is the ability of team members to listen to each other." Glenn M. Parker, Team Players and Teamwork: New Strategies for Developing Successful Collaboration[69]

Team = 24 guys hanging together on the same rope

CHAPTER 5

Building Healthy Relationships

Building Healthy Relationships

A Servant Leader engages in and develops meaningful relationships, promoting involvement to influence.

Although it may take some time to develop Servant Leadership, the benefits are worth it. Sometimes, people want to short-circuit the process of learning to lead well. It takes time and commitment to learn how to...

- seek to serve as Jesus serves.
- value teamwork.
- build healthy relationships.

THE HEART OF SERVANT LEADERSHIP

Let's talk about healthy relationships. We mentioned earlier that the heart of Servant Leadership is neither power nor authority, but *influence.*

Servant Leaders seek to influence the way people think and behave. They point people to Jesus by reminding them that God has an eternal purpose for everyone, just as He did for Jesus.

Servant Leaders do not build a kingdom for themselves. They understand that God has given them an opportunity to influence groups of people so the group can bring glory to God and grace to the lives of others in society.

Servant Leaders have the privilege of influencing people toward a grand goal. Their team members could possibly change the medical profession or the legal system. They may improve educational institutions or revitalize the arts. They could even introduce exciting, innovative products, or maybe reimagine Christian outreach so it serves marginalized men, women, and children more effectively. They may find a way to use technology to advance a message of reconciliation and justice. They might connect farmers and restauranteurs to food banks.

Whatever your calling may be, use your influence as a leader to produce work that makes a difference. You are, in fact, a catalyst for change.

Think about the ordinary men and women you know who influence well in their leadership roles, such as...

+ Athletic coaches expect their players to practice in the pounding rain, in blazing heat, and in blinding snow. When players are tired or frustrated, coaches urge them to keep going, not simply for their own benefit, but for the sake of the team. Coaches ask their players to develop resilience as they strive for victory. In each instance, the coaches model perseverance, working with the players under difficult circumstances so they can excel.

+ Dedicated teachers inspire their students to wrestle with ideas, persist through setbacks, then check and correct their work, thus broadening their understanding so they can exceed their goals. They assign work that forces students to boost critical thinking skills and spark curiosity. They ask students to collaborate and build solid communication skills. They equip students with tools that prepare them for college, career, and life. Likewise, effective teachers view themselves as life-long learners, forever improving their pedagogy and finding inventive ways to engage their students.

+ Pastors and church leaders motivate teams to minister to people at various stages of life, from Sunday Schools and home groups, to men's or women's Bible studies, and interactive ministries to children and youth. Pastors and church leaders rely on teams to greet visitors and check on people who are sick or lonely. They train team members to serve the community through feeding programs and Title 1 school partnerships. Effective churches rely on Servant Leaders to fulfill their mission.

Whether you interface with people in the world of business, medicine, law, education, service industries, nonprofit organizations, or public policy, you have a unique opportunity to lead your team through serving.

Servant Leadership is not a step into greatness. It is greatness.

~ WORTH QUOTING ~

J. Oswald Sanders wrote, "One person can lead others only to the extent that they can influence them."[70]

Author John Maxwell put it this way: "A leader is one who knows the way, goes the way and shows the way." He also said, "If you're leading and no one is following, you're only taking a walk.[71]

SERVANT LEADERSHIP AND PERSONALITY STYLES

Influence has nothing to do with temperament or personality style.

+ *Some leaders are extroverts.* They speak loudly and confidently. They may identify and solve problems quickly. They might read people accurately and engage their team in constructive conversations that steadily drive the organization forward.

+ *Some leaders are introverts.* They project a quiet confidence. In most instances, they seem unflustered when they face trouble.

They know how to quell disputes calmly because they consider all sides of an issue before trying to restore the peace.

- *Some leaders are highly intelligent, even scholarly.* They draw from a deep well of knowledge, relying on a network of experts to help them make decisions. They take time to research an issue and deliberate with informed members of the team.

- *Some leaders are seasoned administrators.* They have managed people for a long time and can draw from a wide range of experiences. Since they tend to interpret change through the lens of history, their team members learn to look for trends.

Regardless of the leader's temperament or style, influence begins with involvement. Servant Leaders cultivate the team's strengths, while addressing weaknesses clearly and with grace. In other words, Servant Leaders invest ample time and energy to foster relationships.

THE IMPORTANCE OF STRONG PEOPLE SKILLS

Consider these quotations from some of the world's most influential individuals who understood the importance of involvement:

- John D. Rockefeller said, "The ability to deal with people is as purchasable a commodity as sugar or coffee and I will pay more for that ability than for any other under the sun."[72]

- Theodore Roosevelt said, "The most important single ingredient in the formula of success is knowing how to get along with people."[73]

- Editors for the American Management Association said, "All leaders must excel at personal proficiency. Without the foundation of trust and credibility, you cannot ask others to follow you. While individuals may have different styles (introvert/extrovert, intuitive/sensing, etc.), an individual leader must be seen as having personal proficiency to engage followers. This is probably the toughest of the five domains to train and some individuals are naturally more capable than others."[74]

- Lee Iacocca, famed former president of Chrysler, once said, "The kiss of death on anyone's personnel file is that they don't know how to get along with people."[75]

• Research conducted by Harvard University, the Carnegie Foundation and Stanford Research Center concluded that "85 percent of job success comes from having well-developed . . . people skills."[76]

As a Servant Leader, it is imperative to be involved with people by building healthy relationships with your team and in the workplace.

SERVANT LEADERS LOOK TO BIBLICAL PRINCIPLES

Paul provides a terrific model of relational ministry. Servant Leaders should refer to this passage often:

You know, brothers and sisters, that our visit to you was not without results. We had previously suffered and been treated outrageously in Philippi, as you know, but with the help of our God we dared to tell you his gospel in the face of strong opposition. For the appeal we make does not spring from error or impure motives, nor are we trying to trick you. On the contrary, we speak as those approved by God to be entrusted with the gospel.

We are not trying to please people but God, who tests our hearts. You know we never used flattery, nor did we put on a mask to cover up greed—God is our witness. We were not looking for praise from people, not from you or anyone else, even though as apostles of Christ we could have asserted our authority.

Instead, we were like young children among you. Just as a nursing mother cares for her children, so we cared for you. Because we loved you so much, we were delighted to share with you not only the gospel of God but our lives as well. Surely you remember, brothers and sisters, our toil and hardship; we worked night and day in order not to be a burden to anyone while we preached the gospel of God to you.

You are witnesses, and so is God, of how holy, righteous and blameless we were among you who believed. For you know that we dealt with each of you as a father deals with his own children, encouraging, comforting and urging you to live lives worthy of God, who calls you into his kingdom and glory (1 Thessalonians 2:1-12 NIV).

This passage outlines five strategic principles regarding Servant Leadership.

1. Servant Leaders intentionally build relationships.

Paul deliberately travelled to Thessalonica; he did not wait for an invitation. In fact, he journeyed to the Greek church amid fierce opposition. See what Paul wrote:

Our visit to you was not without results. We had previously suffered and been treated outrageously in Philippi, as you know, but with the help of our God we dared to tell you his gospel in the face of strong opposition (1 Thessalonians 2:1-2 NIV).

Paul could have waited for the quarrels to subside, or he could have waited for someone else to straighten out the problems. Paul headed *into* the fray, trusting that the Thessalonians would listen to him. He *dared* to declare the gospel, *despite* observable resistance.

Servant Leaders initiate the building of relationships. You must choose to initiate getting involved with people through relationships so that you can influence them.

2. Servant Leaders demonstrate compassion, respect, and wisdom.

Paul understands that the Thessalonians cannot pay him a salary, so he refuses to burden them. Look at his appeal:

Surely you remember, brothers and sisters, our toil and hardship; we worked night and day in order not to be a burden to anyone while we preached the gospel of God to you. You are witnesses, and so is God, of how holy, righteous and blameless we were among you who believed (1 Thessalonians 2:9-10 NIV).

The Apostle addresses potential concerns from the outset. He knows the people will not listen to him if he does not take their financial circumstances into account.

Paul also assumes a parental role with the Thessalonian believers as they grapple with core truths. Rather than scolding them, he demonstrates forbearance, likening himself and his team to nursing mothers whose sole focus are their children. He wrote:

> Just as a nursing mother cares for her children, so we cared for you. Because we loved you so much, we were delighted to share with you not only the gospel of God but our lives as well (1 Thessalonians 2:7-8 NIV).

Then, Paul compares himself and the team to fathers, who help their children mature. He says:

> For you know that we dealt with each of you as a father deals with his own children, encouraging, comforting and urging you to live lives worthy of God, who calls you into his kingdom and glory (1 Thessalonians 2:11-12 NIV).

You must look for proactive opportunities to build meaningful relationships. Take the initiative. You could say, "Hey, let's go to lunch and talk about your project." Or, you might say, "Let's pray this through. Let's try to find a productive solution together."

Servant Leaders tune their "spiritual antennas" to the "radio frequency" of other people. Like Paul, they listen carefully, reading between the lines, asking the right questions. Since they are perceptive *and* compassionate, they know *when* and *how* to impart wisdom. They know when to extend grace, and they know when to hold someone accountable. In short, they lead the team from a position of love and trust.

3. Servant Leaders demonstrate authentic affection and concern for others.

Servant Leaders build healthy relationships with people through consistent fellowship and wholesome affection. Look at this verse again. Paul wrote:

Because we loved you so much, we were delighted to share with you not only the gospel of God but our lives as well (1 Thessalonians 2:8 NIV).

Another translation puts it this way:

So, being affectionately desirous of you, we were ready to share with you not only the gospel of God but also our own selves, because you had become very dear to us (1 Thessalonians 2:8 ESV).

"You had become very dear to us." A detached, self-absorbed leader would never say these words. Only a Servant Leader can express sincere affection, particularly within the context of intense conflict and confusion.

Paul is neither aloof nor secretive. He does not travel with an entourage. He never puts on airs. He does not expect special treatment. Instead, he identifies the most pressing needs and addresses them with humility, wisdom, and grace.

~ WORTH QUOTING ~

Theologian John Stott says,

Paul's ministry in Thessalonica had been public. It was exercised in the open before God and human beings for he had nothing whatever to hide. Happy are those Christian leaders today who hate hypocrisy and love integrity, who have nothing to conceal or be ashamed of, who are well known for who and what they are, and who are able to appeal without fear to God and the public as their witnesses! We need more transparency and openness of this kind today.[77]

I urge you to embrace authenticity and accountability among your leadership team and with people.

4. Servant Leaders affirm everyone on the team when they can.

Paul implores the Thessalonians to "live lives worthy of God, who calls you into his kingdom and glory" (1 Thessalonians 2:12 NIV).

Notice the tone here. Paul does not reprimand the Thessalonians. He does not harass or embarrass them. Instead, Paul encourages them to forgive, cooperate, appreciate, and accommodate one another. He's affirming them!

My father was a wonderful example of affirmation. I played baseball in high school and college, and I fondly remember that Dad made great effort to attend the games. I could always hear him in the stands, yelling, "Way to go! Great hit! Nice play! You'll get them next time!"

I recall one game in particular: my worst game in high school. For the life of me, I could not hit a thing. I could neither field nor throw the ball well. It was humiliating. Miraculously, we won the game, but not because I played well. When I returned home, my dad was sitting on the couch. As soon as I walked through the door, he jumped up, threw his arms around me, and said, "I'm proud of you."

It has been well over sixty years since that night, but my father's response deeply impacted me. He showed me that authentic love looks beyond the outcome. Authentic love sees the person, despite flaws and failures.

You must remember that people in crisis need affirmation and may require help or guidance, but they also need encouragement. As a Servant Leader, learn to recognize these moments as opportunities to say, "You are not alone. God is here, and so am I."

Affirm your team members whenever they succeed and also when they struggle. Affirm your people because they are on your team. *Affirmation sticks!*

5. Servant Leaders build healthy, fruitful relationships that reflect their integrity.

Paul urges the Thessalonians to consider the example that he and his companions set:

> For the appeal we make does not spring from error or impure motives, nor are we trying to trick you. On the contrary, we speak as those approved by God to be entrusted with the gospel. We are not trying to please people but God, who tests our hearts. You know we never used flattery, nor did we put on a mask to cover up greed—God is our witness. We were not looking for praise from people, not from you or anyone else, even though as apostles of Christ we could have asserted our authority (1 Thessalonians 2:3-6 NIV).

Paul values personal integrity. He understands his responsibility to share the gospel faithfully. He rejects the temptation to manipulate his brothers and sisters. He rejects flattery and greed.

Allow your team to see how you live. Let them compare your words and actions with biblical standards. Naturally, you will fall short from time to time, but your willingness to admit your faults and to make corrections will highlight your integrity. Allow the Spirit to radiate decency and selflessness through you.

THE "LEGS" THAT SUPPORT A HEALTHY RELATIONSHIP

Servant Leaders invest in people, fostering trust, sharing responsibility, and affirming others, while promoting an atmosphere of credibility and integrity.

A team with flourishing relationships will reflect balance, like a chair that has four perfectly balanced legs. Each leg helps to bear the weight of the person sitting in the chair. If one leg is missing or damaged, the chair might collapse. Likewise, healthy relationships include these four essential "legs":

1. TRUST: Healthy relationships depend on trust.

Trust is the most important characteristic, but it is also the most fragile one.

~ DID YOU KNOW? ~

According to entrepreneur and global business leader, Marissa Levin, "polarizing, destructive behaviors" lead to alienation and frustration, even prompting some workers to seek employment elsewhere. She says that leaders break trust when they exhibit the following traits and behaviors:[78]

- Inauthenticity
- False Promises
- Ambiguity
- One-Way Communication
- Personal Agendas/Ego-Driven Leadership
- Anger
- Refusing to Delegate/Empower
- An Attitude of Superiority/Lack of Appreciation
- Playing Favorites

Servant Leadership requires trust, especially since team members sacrifice their time, energy, perhaps their future, to fulfill the leader's vision.

You must take your responsibility seriously, and you should do everything you can to earn your colleagues' trust. Here is how:

- Be reliable. When you make a commitment, honor your word. Complete tasks with excellence. Arrive at meetings on time and honor your deadlines; a willingness to manage your time demonstrates respect for other people's time.

- Know when to keep a confidence. Confidentiality is crucial in leadership. Seek input whenever it is appropriate, and *always* work through the proper channels. Respect the privacy of your team members and avoid gossip at all cost.

- Commit yourself to the truth—even if telling the truth endangers your vision. Speak the truth in love because you care about your team members (Ephesians 4:15).

+ Prove that you are loyal. When a member of the team is floundering, pull up a chair, offer to listen and help.

+ Place your confidence in the Lord Jesus. Recognize your own flaws and limitations. Depend on the Lord Jesus for direction, clarity, correction, and wisdom.

2. LOVE: Healthy relationships depend on love.

It may feel strange to talk about love in the context of the workplace, but a godly commitment to love points to stability and an enduring desire to see other people thrive.

You will strengthen your team—and your organization—by responding with caring love. Show up with genuine love, even if no one else will.

Use your position to care for others, like the Good Samaritan. When you identify a need, respond with compassion. When appropriate, enlist the help of qualified people to help.

3. RESPECT: Healthy relationships depend on respect.

Effective Servant Leaders respect their peers, managers, assistants, customers, clients, supporters, custodians, and board members. They respect all people, regardless of the individual's position in the organization or station in life.

According to a 2014 report, half of the world's employees said they felt that their boss did not respect them. Yet, the same report suggests that productivity, health, and enjoyment in the workplace escalate dramatically when an employer demonstrates genuine respect.[79]

Find ways to show your team how much you appreciate them. Acknowledge effort and affirm grit. Value diversity and encourage inclusion.

~ WORTH READING AGAIN ~

Luke records Jesus' story of the Good Samaritan:
On one occasion an expert in the law stood up to test Jesus.
"Teacher," he asked, "what must I do to inherit eternal life?"
"What is written in the Law?" he replied. "How do you read it?"

He answered, "'Love the Lord your God with all your heart and
with all your soul and with all your strength and with all your
mind'; and, 'Love your neighbor as yourself.'"

"You have answered correctly," Jesus replied.
"Do this and you will live."

But he wanted to justify himself, so he asked Jesus,
"And who is my neighbor?"

In reply Jesus said: "A man was going down from Jerusalem to
Jericho, when he was attacked by robbers. They stripped him
of his clothes, beat him and went away, leaving him half dead.
A priest happened to be going down the same road, and when
he saw the man, he passed by on the other side. So too, a
Levite, when he came to the place and saw him, passed by on
the other side. But a Samaritan, as he traveled, came where the
man was; and when he saw him, he took pity on him. He went
to him and bandaged his wounds, pouring on oil and wine.
Then he put the man on his own donkey, brought him to an inn
and took care of him. The next day he took out two denarii and
gave them to the innkeeper. 'Look after him,' he said, 'and when
I return, I will reimburse you for any extra expense you may
have.'

"Which of these three do you think was a neighbor to the man
who fell into the hands of robbers?"

The expert in the law replied, "The one who had mercy on him."
Jesus told him, "Go and do likewise" (Luke 10:25-37 NIV).

4. KNOWLEDGE AND UNDERSTANDING: Healthy relationships depend on knowledge and understanding.

Servant Leaders know the members of their team, and they understand how they think.

John recorded Jesus' words:

> "I am the good shepherd. The good shepherd lays down his life for the sheep. The hired hand is not the shepherd and does not own the sheep. So when he sees the wolf coming, he abandons the sheep and runs away. Then the wolf attacks the flock and scatters it. The man runs away because he is a hired hand and cares nothing for the sheep.

> "I am the good shepherd; I know my sheep and my sheep know me—just as the Father knows me and I know the Father—and I lay down my life for the sheep" (John 10:11-15 NIV).

Strive to know your team members personally. Discover how to motivate them in a way that is meaningful to them. Follow Jesus' example of sacrificial love so that everyone on the team feels valued.

Like a stable chair, healthy relationships support the "weight" of an organization. As a Servant Leader, you must make sure that each "leg" functions properly.

Chapter 5 Review
"Building Healthy Relationships"

- The heart of Servant Leadership is influence.
- Servant Leadership is not limited to personality styles, intelligence, or experience.
- Servant Leaders must develop strong people skills.
- Servant Leaders look to biblical principles.
- There are five strategic principles regarding Servant Leadership:
  - » Intentionally build relationships.
  - » Demonstrate compassion, respect, and wisdom.
  - » Demonstrate authentic affection and concern for others.
  - » Affirm everyone on the team.
  - » Build healthy, fruitful relationships.
- There are four "legs" that support a healthy relationship:
  - » Trust (the most fragile, yet the most crucial)
  - » Love (the most enduring)
  - » Respect or Honor (the most neglected)
  - » Knowledge and Understanding (the one that takes the longest)

CHAPTER 6

Understanding Power

Understanding Power

A Servant Leader uses his or her power for the benefit of others, not self-benefit, promoting an ability to influence.

You have probably encountered a leader who had the power to execute a plan and yet you saw investors, key colleagues, talented employees, or church leaders hesitate. What went wrong? The leader may have had an impressive resume and ample resources, but something was missing.

People waver if they believe that the leader will misuse his or her power. They may question the leader's motives. They may doubt that the leader can garner enough support to fulfill promises and meet deadlines.

At the heart of these objections is a leader's failure to establish trust. Somewhere down the line, the leader neglected to prove that he or she understands the proper use of the leadership position.

Ineffective leaders equate power with control, so they use their position to bully and manipulate their people. The result is an erosion of trust that damages relationships and organizations.

A wise Servant Leader, however, understands that power is a privilege, not a prize. God has given the leader power to serve people, not dominate them.

THE POWER TO . . .?

Suppose a person builds a mansion, furnishing it with *every-thing* the individual could ever need or want. The house has spacious rooms and closets, designer furniture, thick carpet, polished floors, and art adorning the walls. It features a swimming pool, a tennis court, and an in-home theater with a state-of-the-art screen and sound system. It has a weight room and a bowling alley. The house has a chef's kitchen, digital appliances, a fully stocked pantry, stunning tableware. It is perfect for entertaining. The house is truly a showcase.

Now, imagine the owners that move into the home. They thoroughly enjoy new luxuries and conveniences. They fill the home with personal possessions, clothing, cars, and so forth. They take pleasure in the amenities—the pool, the tennis court, and all the entertainment options.

Then, one day, the owners decide they don't need to live in such an opulent house. They don't mind the luxury, but they're ready to leave it behind. Instead, they move into a small apartment in the poorest part of town. With money from the sale of the house, they feed the hungry, clothe the naked, provide medical care for sick people, come alongside weak and lonely men and women.

A dramatic change has occurred. The owners have emptied themselves of the benefits of wealth so they could serve the needs of others. They have relinquished something valuable to serve others.

That is in small part what Jesus did when He came to the earth. And that is precisely what Servant Leaders do.

SERVANT LEADERS LIVE TO GIVE

Servant Leaders live to give. That's our motto, our creed.

Servant Leaders combine their power with generosity. Indeed, Servant Leaders *live to give*. They give vision, wisdom, encouragement, and reinforcement, not for their own glory but to help other people flourish.

In other words, Servant Leaders view power as a tool by which they can serve people.

By living to give, Servant Leaders identify needs and serve from a heart of compassion. They allocate resources and implement plans that benefit people and communities.

Servant Leaders also understand the importance of biblical standards, so they model them for their followers to emulate in life and work. Leadership is not for the faint-hearted, but godly leadership is rewarding nonetheless, especially since it reflects the character and purposes of Christ Jesus.

No one steps into a position of leadership thinking, "I hope I fail. I plan to make poor decisions that will damage my organization." The trouble usually starts when a leader ignores sound advice and starts looking for shortcuts, or when the leader refuses to stand on conviction.

By contrast, a Servant Leader commits to biblical standards, using his or her power for the common good, not for personal gain. The leader promotes worthwhile goals, despite obstacles and setbacks, guiding people with discernment and grace.

Since no one succeeds alone, an effective Servant Leader invests time and energy to help people thrive in all areas of life. That means "living to give."

Servant Leaders faithfully share their vision so that men and women from all walks of life can help them fulfill Christ's calling. Servant Leadership is not "give and take," but "give and serve."

~ DID YOU KNOW? ~

Myron Rush argues that a Servant Leader must

- Stand on conviction, against public opinion if necessary.
- Be willing to risk failure.
- Master his or her emotions.
- Live above reproach.
- Be willing to make difficult, unpopular decisions.
- Sacrifice personal interests for the sake of the team.
- Strive for excellence, never settling for "good enough."
- Remember that people are more important than goals and possessions.
- Maintain balance in all areas of life, including family, work, church, and friends.[80]

THE POWER TO INFLUENCE

For many leaders, power is intoxicating and addictive, inducing them to focus their attention on their emerging "kingdom." Their aim is to increase and sustain their power. Typically, these leaders equate power with dominance, which frequently results in frustration, regression, or failure within the organization.

By contrast, Servant Leaders understand the proper use of power.

Servant Leaders view their power as an avenue by which they can influence the way individuals view themselves, other people, and society. Rather than envisaging power as a goal, Servant Leaders regard power as a responsibility.

Consider this definition:

POWER is the ability to influence people to do something or to change in some way, whether they want to or not.

Servant Leaders understand that they possess the power to influence people in a positive way. As a result, they foster an atmosphere of trust that propels the team toward harmony and creative cooperation.

Servant Leaders can shape the culture of a business or institution by promoting integrity, respect, and accountability. By using their power to unite people, they encourage their followers to collaborate and produce meaningful work.

THE ALLURE OF POWER

When I watch television, I use a remote control to turn the television on and off, change the channels, increase or decrease the volume, reformat the size of the picture, adjust the colors, or add closed captioning. With the remote control, I can rent or buy a movie, and shop online. If I want, I can watch two shows simultaneously. The remote control *empowers* me to mold my entertainment options to suit my taste. Frankly, I love my remote control. I appreciate its power and the ease with which I can make changes.

My wife, however, hates the remote control. She feels annoyed when I use the remote to select shows without her input. She feels that I am using the remote control for my own pleasure...and she is *right*. It's true. I do allow this poor exercise of power in my own living room because I'm generally exercising it when I'm *alone*.

In your areas of leadership, people are not at your beck and call like a remote control, and you cannot over-exert your power because it's not your living room. Many leaders confuse this.

The allure of power can draw leaders off course, blinding them to the real goal—a life that pleases God. They may fancy themselves as superior to other individuals, assuming they deserve perks and accolades. Nothing could be further from the truth. Consider Jesus. He possessed absolute power, yet He never allowed the allure of power to weaken His resolve.

GUARDING THE HEART

If you hope to be an effective Servant Leader, you must guard your heart against the allure of power. Solomon warns:

Above all else, guard your heart, for everything you do flows from it (Proverbs 4:23 NIV).

Likewise, Henri Nouwen describes the painful struggle that many Christian leaders face when it comes to power:

> One of the greatest ironies of the history of Christianity is that its leaders constantly give in to the temptation of power—political power, military power, economic power, or moral and spiritual power—even though they continued to speak in the name of Jesus....
>
> The long painful history of the Church is the history of people ever and again tempted to choose power over love, control over the cross, being a leader over being led. One thing is clear: the temptation of power is greatest when intimacy is a threat. Much Christian leadership is exercised by people who do not know how to develop healthy, intimate relationships and have opted for power and control instead.[81]

Jesus describes authentic power in terms of service and love. Guarding the heart includes accountability. Leaders should have a trusted group of friends and counselors who will hold them accountable to God's leadership preference.

Dr. Nouwen wrote:

> The leadership about which Jesus speaks is radically different from the leadership offered by the world. It is servant leadership in which the leader is a vulnerable servant who needs the people as much as they need him.[82]
>
> Finally, leaders must spend time in the Word and prayer. This combination of community, Bible study, and prayer can help leaders guard their hearts against the ever-present pull toward worldly power.

THE NEED FOR A NEW UNDERSTANDING OF POWER

Jesus deals with questions surrounding power while He and His disciples are walking to Jerusalem. Jesus knows when he arrives that vocal adversaries will arrest Him, torture Him, and put Him on trial. Eventually, they will call for His death. So, as He travels to the city, He is thinking about one thing: a cross.

> As the time approached for him to be taken up to heaven, Jesus *resolutely set out* for Jerusalem (NIV). Another version puts it this way: When the days drew near for him to be taken up, he *set his face* to go to Jerusalem (Luke 9:51 ESV).

The disciples, however, are not thinking about a cross. Instead, they are bickering over their importance. James and John, the sons of Zebedee, approach Jesus to ask a favor. Would He allow them to sit on either side of Him in the Kingdom? In other words, would He give them the seats of honor when He establishes His reign?

Jesus is focused on a cross. James and John are focused on personal glory and thrones, titles and positions of power.

This scenario seems familiar in our current culture. Many leaders want to form massive corporations. Some leaders seek to build large charities, megachurches, or found schools that attract elite students from prominent families.

Look at the passage:

> They were on their way up to Jerusalem, with Jesus leading the way, and the disciples were astonished, while those who followed were afraid. Again, he took the Twelve aside and told them what was going to happen to him. "We are going up to Jerusalem," he said, "and the Son of Man will be delivered over to the chief priests and the teachers of the law. They will condemn him to death and will hand him

over to the Gentiles, who will mock him and spit on him, flog him and kill him. Three days later he will rise."

Then James and John, the sons of Zebedee, came to him. "Teacher," they said, "we want you to do for us whatever we ask."

"What do you want me to do for you?" he asked.

They replied, "Let one of us sit at your right and the other at your left in your glory."

"You don't know what you are asking," Jesus said. "Can you drink the cup I drink or be baptized with the baptism I am baptized with?"

"We can," they answered.

Jesus said to them, "You will drink the cup I drink and be baptized with the baptism I am baptized with, but to sit at my right or left is not for me to grant. These places belong to those for whom they have been prepared."

When the ten heard about this, they became indignant with James and John. Jesus called them together and said, "You know that those who are regarded as rulers of the Gentiles lord it over them, and their high officials exercise authority over them. Not so with you. Instead, whoever wants to become great among you must be your servant, and whoever wants to be first must be slave of all. For even the Son of Man did not come to be served, but to serve, and to give his life as a ransom for many" (Mark 10:32-45 NIV).

As soon as the rest of the disciples heard about James and John's request, they "became indignant." They were infuriated because James and John beat them to the punch. They were jealous, and in that very moment, Jesus called them together to teach them about service and greatness.

POWER LEADERSHIP VS. SERVANT LEADERSHIP

Jesus' idea of greatness flies in the face of conventional thinking. He says that power and greatness flow from *humility* to serve others. Servant Leadership contrasts sharply with flawed Power Leadership models. Look at what Jesus said:

> "You know that those who are regarded as rulers of the Gentiles lord it over them, And their high officials exercise authority over them" (Mark 10:42 NIV).

Power Leaders "lord it over" their followers, "exercising their authority" to pursue their own goals. Although these phrases differ in the Greek text, they carry the same meaning: ruling over people for a leader's own personal benefit, rather than serving them.

CHARACTERISTICS OF A POWER LEADER

In short, Power Leaders use their position to attain greatness and to control people; the result can be demoralizing and fruitless.

As leaders learn to guard their hearts, they must move away from Power Leadership. Here are a few traits that characterize Power Leaders:

+ They strive to control people and circumstances.
+ They seek prominence and fame.
+ They advance their own interests over the interests of other people.
+ They are willing to manipulate, intimidate, malign, or abuse people to achieve their goals.
+ They will fire or demote individuals who oppose them.
+ They refuse to share responsibility or glory with colleagues and subordinates; they have trouble trusting others, even though they demand loyalty from the team.

"NOT SO WITH YOU"

Jesus urges the disciples to view power differently; He starts with four simple words: *"Not so with you"* (Mark 10:43 NIV).

Jesus explains that Servant Leaders want to achieve greatness, but not for themselves; they are *sacrificial* leaders, working for the good in others, not themselves. They seek the greater good for another person's benefit.

Notice that Jesus does not scold the disciples for being ambitious. Ambition itself is not wrong. The problem stems from wrong motives, including a quest for power, fame, or wealth.

Jesus redefines ambition, explaining that effective leaders set their desires aside to serve others. It is focusing not inwardly on yourself, but outwardly, focusing on others and their good.

Jesus talks about power in the context of His Kingdom, applying His authority and vision to minister to individuals.

> "Not so with you. Instead, whoever wants to become great among you must be your servant, and whoever wants to be first must be slave of all. For even the Son of Man did not come to be served, but to serve, and to give his life as a ransom for many" (Mark 10:43-45 NIV).

By viewing power from Jesus' perspective, Servant Leaders understand their role more clearly.

CHARACTERISTICS OF A SERVANT LEADER

By studying Jesus' example in Mark chapter 10, we also see the contrast between the Power Leader who tries to control people and the Servant Leader who loves and serves people. Consider the following traits, which portray the Servant Leader as one who...

+ values transparency and accessibility, striving to listen well.

+ shares the spotlight by allowing team members to contribute to decisions.

+ mentors the team, giving people an opportunity to build healthy relationships.

+ combines power and authority with responsibility and accountability.

+ demonstrates integrity from a heart of humility.

These characteristics reveal authentic, Christlike character. Leadership experts Warren Bennis and Robert Townsend believe that "neither science nor formula will produce a leader; leadership is a matter of character."[83]

Note that Servant Leaders embrace integrity and humility. These traits enable risking transparency and accessibility as they listen to others. These traits also enable sharing the spotlight, mentoring the team, and building healthy relationships. They pave the way for Servant Leaders to combine power with responsibility and accountability.

The Hebrew term for *integrity* extends beyond honesty, presenting instead the idea of "wholeness, uprightness, being ethically sound."[84]

Jesus was the perfect example of integrity as He interacted with people from every station of life, including those who were outcasts. As the perfect Servant Leader, He modeled integrity daily, exhorting His followers to do the same.

Servant Leaders should model integrity and humility so they can build healthy relationships, enabling them to mentor people well. All leaders have power; the key is to use power responsibly—not for the good of the leader, but for the good of those he or she is leading. That is the supreme difference between a Power Leader and a Servant Leader.

USING GOD-GIVEN POWER RESPONSIBLY

Peter Drucker famously stated, "Management has no power. Management has only responsibility."[85]

Although various forms of leadership may exist in an organization, a Servant Leader exercises power through service and influence. Power is used properly when the Servant Leader submits to the authority and interests of the Lord Jesus.

~ DID YOU KNOW? ~

According to leadership expert Bernard M. Bass, there are five general types of power:

1. **Expert Power** comes from the leader's depth of knowledge, skill, or wisdom; while Expert Power relies on understanding, this type of leader may view his or her opinion more highly than everyone else's.

2. **Referent Po**wer suggests that the leader's power derives from the follower's desire to identify with the leader and find acceptance; in some instances, a person who relies on Referent Power to lead can become coercive and domineering.

3. **Reward Power** refers to a leadership style that encourages desired conduct through public praise, bonuses, and other incentives; obviously, team members respond well to various forms of encouragement, but Servant Leaders should be wary of manipulating workers through the use of rewards alone.

4. **Power** denotes control by giving or withholding rewards and penalizing workers who fail to live up to the leader's standards; in most instances, team members fear this leader, which results in a loss of respect and motivation. It is important to note that coercive leaders may be overtly brutal or subtly manipulative; in either case, the objective is the same.

5. **Legitimate Powe**r might be called "Position Power" because it focuses on the group to establish the organization's norms and expectations; hence, the standards apply to the designated leader and for the team.[86]

Chapter 6 Review
"Understanding Power"

- Servants Leaders use their power to serve people, not dominate them.

- Servant Leaders live to give; they use their power to meet needs, cast vision, share wisdom, or encourage people who are struggling.

- Servant Leaders have the power to influence the way individuals see themselves, other people, and society.

- POWER is the ability to influence people to do something or to change in some way, whether they want to or not.

- The allure of power can draw leaders off course, blinding them to the real goal: a life that pleases God.

- A Servant Leader must guard his or her heart against the allure of power.

- A Servant Leader should recognize his or her need for a biblical understanding of power.

- Power Leaders stand in stark contrast to Servant Leaders.

- There are six characteristics of a Power Leader:

  » They strive to control people and circumstances.

  » They seek prominence and fame.

  » They advance their own interests over the interests of other people.

  » They are willing to manipulate, intimidate, malign, or abuse people to achieve their goals.

  » They will fire or demote individuals who oppose them.

  » They refuse to share responsibility or glory with colleagues and subordinates; they have trouble trusting others, even though they demand loyalty from the team.

- Jesus tells His disciples that the world praises Power Leaders, but that is "not so with you."
  - » Biblical leadership is sacrificial.
  - » Biblical leadership loves people, despite their circumstances.
  - » Biblical leadership works for the greater good.
  - » Ambition itself is not wrong, but wrong motives can spoil healthy ambition.
  - » Jesus wants leaders to help people who cannot help themselves.
- There are five characteristics of a Servant Leader:
  - » Valuing transparency and accessibility, striving to listen well
  - » Sharing the spotlight by allowing team members to contribute to decisions
  - » Mentoring the team, giving people an opportunity to build healthy relationships
  - » Combining power and authority with responsibility and accountability
  - » Demonstrating integrity from a heart of humility
- Power is used properly when the Servant Leader submits to the authority and interests of the Lord Jesus.

CHAPTER 7

Understanding Authority

Understanding Authority

A Servant Leader submits to the authority and interests of the Lord Jesus Christ, promoting the right to lead.

Some leaders believe that authority is a natural extension of power, but this is not always the case. As history attests, persuasive individuals can impose their power over others, overstepping their authority.

Servant Leaders realize that authority is a *privilege*. Indeed, *biblical authority* lays the groundwork for healthy decisions that shape the organization.

Consider this definition:

AUTHORITY is the right to exercise power so that other people can thrive.

Imagine an ordinary thirty-year-old woman standing in the middle of a busy street. She sees cars rushing past her. She walks into the middle of the road and holds up her hand. What would happen? Potentially, several things could occur:

- A driver might accidentally run her over.
- Cars might crash into each other as they try to avoid the woman and each other.
- Cars might veer off road, plowing into pedestrians and buildings.

In any event, there would surely be confusion.

However, what if the woman is a police officer? What if she strides into the street and holds up her hand, signaling for cars to stop? What would happen then? Most likely, the cars would slow to a halt. Why? The drivers would see the officer's symbols of authority, including her uniform and badge, and they would respond accordingly.

People typically acknowledge symbols of authority, such as titles, uniforms, or the size and location of an individual's office. Yet, symbols only go so far. Workers respect leaders who combine authority with serving, wisdom, compassion, and practical action.

A BIBLICAL VIEW OF AUTHORITY

Where do Servant Leaders get their authority?

Do they have authority because they hold a leadership title or position?

Is it because they know how to redirect people, telling others what they can and cannot do?

Is it because the leader has a strong personality?

Is it because he or she has skills, knowledge, or acumen?

Is it because the leader has money and connections?

Is it because the leader has experience managing groups of people?

While certain leadership traits may be helpful, the Servant Leader understands that real authority comes from the Lord Jesus Christ.

Authority is the right to exercise power. An effective Servant Leader uses his or her authority to help other people *thrive*. Rather than simply delegating tasks, the Servant Leader has the right to guide team members so that everyone has a better chance of succeeding.

Sometimes, the team needs specific direction. In such cases, the Servant Leader should use his or her authority to provide clarity.

For instance, imagine a team gathering in a small office. The leader looks around and says, "I'm glad you are all here, but we need more room. We are too crowded here. We will have to move the group to a new spot." The leader has authority to tell the team what to do. He or she has the *right* to exercise power in this situation.

By contrast, ineffective leaders confuse power with authority. They often demand and cajole. In some instances, they deceive, even manipulate, their team. They may threaten their colleagues or make empty promises. These responses can seriously damage the organization and destroy trust.

Author Howard E. Butt, Jr., said, "Christ came to introduce a new kind of authority. The crisis of the age is the authority crisis."[87]

When a leader submits to Christ's authority and His interests, he or she can empower others to exercise authority in their respective leadership roles.

According to Scripture, there are two ways that a Servant Leader gains authority.

1. Submit your life and leadership to the authority of the Lord Jesus.

Paul wrote to the Corinthians:

> For Christ's love compels us, because we are convinced that one died for all, and therefore all died. And he died for all, that those who live should no longer live for themselves but for him who died for them and was raised again (2 Corinthians 5:14-15 NIV).

Jesus Christ alone is sovereign. Only He has the final authority over our lives.

Remember, you are reflecting the lordship of Jesus in all that you do. As you submit to Christ's authority, you will find the authority you need to exercise your power.

2. Submit your interests to Jesus' interests.

Paul told the Corinthians:

For what we preach is not ourselves, but Jesus Christ as Lord, and ourselves as your servants for Jesus' sake (2 Corinthians 4:5 NIV).

Jesus told people to "seek first his kingdom and his righteousness, and all these things will be given to you as well" (Matthew 6:33 NIV). In accordance with this verse, look at this list of Jesus' primary interests:

+ Christ is interested in God's glory (John 17:4).

+ Christ is interested in proper worship (Matthew 21:12-17; John 2:13-22).

+ Christ is interested in the Great Commission (Matthew 28:16-20; Mark 16:14-16; Luke 24:44-49; John 20:19-23; Acts 1:8).

+ Christ is interested in confronting sin (Matthew 18:15-20).

+ Christ is interested in restoring sinning saints (Matthew 18:15-16).

+ Christ is interested in correcting competitive leadership (Mark 10:43-45).

+ Christ is interested in stable marriages (Matthew 5:31-32; 19:3-12).

+ Christ is interested in having authoritative leadership (Matthew 18:18-20; 28:20; Mark 6:7; John 20:21-23).

The degree to which a Servant Leader lives out the character qualities of spirituality (which is, God-ward), integrity (inward), and humility (outward) will be the degree to which people permit themselves to be influenced.

Dr. John Stott wisely observed:

The authority by which the Christian leader leads is not power, but love, not force, but example, not coercion, but reasoned persuasion. Leaders have power, but power is safe only in the hands of those who humble themselves to serve.[88]

Chapter 7 Review
"Understanding Authority"

+ Servant Leaders realize that authority is a *privilege*; indeed, *biblical authority* lays the groundwork for healthy decisions that shape the organization.

+ *AUTHORITY is the right to exercise power so that other people can thrive.*

+ Servant Leaders need a biblical view of authority.

  » An effective Servant Leader initiates action so that everyone has a better chance of succeeding.

  » Servant Leaders set an example of transparency, looking for ways to inspire their team.

  » They provide clear direction and encourage the team.

+ Servant Leaders submit to the Lord Jesus, thus empowering others to exercise authority in their respective leadership roles.

+ There are two ways that a Servant Leader gains authority:

  » A Servant Leader must submit his or her life to the authority of the Lord Jesus.

  » A Servant Leader must submit his or her interests to Jesus' interests.

+ The degree to which a Servant Leader lives out the character qualities of spirituality (which is, God-ward), integrity (inward), and humility (outward) will be the degree to which people permit themselves to be influenced.

CHAPTER 8

Embracing Humility

CHAPTER 8

Embracing Humility

*Servant Leaders live in humility by promoting
others above themselves.*

Learning to be an effective Servant Leader is a process, a *daily* process, and it will take a lifetime to complete. Nevertheless, every time you take a step in the right direction, you make progress, largely because you are changing the way you think and lead, forming productive, life-giving habits.

So far, we have examined Servant Leadership in the context of the following principles:

- Servant Leaders think like Jesus by relinquishing what keeps us back from serving.

- Servant Leaders live like Jesus, by doing menial tasks when necessary.

- Servant Leaders value teamwork, knowing that no one succeeds alone.

- Servant Leaders build healthy relationships, realizing that relationships are at the heart of leadership.

- Servant Leaders understand power enables them to influence followers so that those following their leadership can grow, mature, and thrive.

- Servant Leaders understand authority gives them the right to exercise power to lead and serve well.

The last principle shows us another path to effectiveness:

+ Servant Leaders understand that humility *energizes* them.

HUMILITY AS A STRENGTH

As we already observed, no quality describes Servant Leadership better than humility, and Jesus, the perfect Servant Leader, invites us to emulate His life:

> "Come to me, all you who are weary and burdened, and I will give you rest. Take my yoke upon you and learn from me, for I am gentle and humble in heart, and you will find rest for your souls. For my yoke is easy and my burden is light" (Matthew 11:28-30 NIV).

Jesus gives us a beautiful picture of a leader who humbles Himself to serve people who cannot help themselves. It is interesting to note that the only time Jesus described Himself was when He said, "Learn from me, for I am gentle and humble in heart" (Matthew 11:29 NIV).

Consider the following definition of humility:

HUMILITY means putting others first and downplaying one's personal desires. Humility seeks to benefit everyone else.

+ Humility is thinking less of yourself and thinking more of others.

+ Humility says, "I understand that you have interests and so do I. Nevertheless, I am willing to consider your interests above my own."

+ Humility chooses the "downward plunge," as it were, to elevate another person.

This is precisely what Jesus did. Read what Paul wrote:

> Who, being in very nature God, did not consider equality with God something to be used to his own advantage; rather, he made himself nothing by taking the very nature of a servant, being made in human likeness. And being found in

appearance as a man, he humbled himself by becoming obedient to death—even death on a cross (Philippians 2:6-8 NIV).

Although Jesus is God, fully deserving honor and worship, He emptied Himself on our behalf:

+ Jesus yielded His divine privileges.
+ Jesus made Himself nothing.
+ He became a man.
+ He became a servant.
+ He humbled Himself by dying on a cross.

That is the "downward plunge." Servant Leaders who emulate Jesus, empty themselves of rank and privilege. They lay aside their preferences so that others can thrive.

Embracing the "mind of Christ" is a life-long *process*. You will probably progress in stages, developing habits that allow you to practice humility more consistently. Paul shows us how to humble ourselves:

Do nothing out of selfish ambition or vain conceit. Rather, in humility value others above yourselves, not looking to your own interests but each of you to the interests of the others (Philippians 2:3-4 NIV).

FOUR STEPS TOWARD A "DOWNWARD PLUNGE" TO GREATNESS

According to Paul's message to the Philippians, you must develop consistency in several areas.

Step One:
Do nothing from selfishness or empty conceit.
Philippians 2:3

Many people have a "me first" attitude at home, work, and society, using words, such as *I, me, my, myself,* and *mine*. They rarely talk about *your* success or *our* efforts. Instead, they promote themselves whenever they get the chance. They have erected a shrine to themselves, and they invite everyone else to worship at that shrine.

Selfishness and conceit lie at the root of many family arguments, in which individuals declare, "I know more than you. Do what I say. I do not like your idea. My way is better." Too often, families experience devastating fractures that result in grudges and recriminations. It would be healthier if family members could set aside their selfishness and humble themselves instead.

Leaders who insist on having their way all the time risk damaging important relationships with family members, friends, and business associates. You may recall a time when you watched a tyrannical boss manipulate, bully, and demean employees until they revolted. Paul warns leaders to avoid such destructive behavior.

Break the "me first" habit through death. Selfishness and conceit flow from the heart. While it is important to think about your behavior, simply willing yourself to change is not enough. Reading your Bible and praying throughout the day are helpful. Good intentions are nice. But you must address the source of the problem. You must die to yourself.

You must believe that you died with Jesus Christ. The Bible says that when Jesus died on the cross, you died with Him. Here are a few examples from Paul's letters to the first-century Christians:

+ For if we have been united with him in a death like his, we will certainly also be united with him in a resurrection like his. For we know that our old self was crucified with him so that the body ruled by sin might be done away with, that we should no longer be slaves to sin—because anyone who has died has been set free from sin. Now if we died with Christ, we believe that we will also live with him (Romans 6:5-8 NIV).

+ I have been crucified with Christ and I no longer live, but Christ lives in me. The life I now live in the body, I live by faith in the Son of God, who loved me and gave himself for me (Galatians 2:20 NIV).

• Here is a trustworthy saying: If we died with him, we will also live with him; if we endure, we will also reign with him (2 Timothy 2:11-12a NIV).

Identifying yourself with Jesus' death means that you understand that He alone is the source of your transformation. Paul wrote:

"Therefore, if anyone is in Christ, the new creation has come: The old has gone, the new is here" (2 Corinthians 5:17 NIV).

Jesus has taken your old life, with its sin, selfishness, and conceit, and dealt with it through the power of the Cross.

Paul continues:

All this is from God, who reconciled us to himself through Christ and gave us the ministry of reconciliation: that God was reconciling the world to himself in Christ, not counting people's sins against them. And he has committed to us the message of reconciliation. We are therefore Christ's ambassadors, as though God were making his appeal through us. We implore you on Christ's behalf: Be reconciled to God. God made him who had no sin to be sin for us, so that in him we might become the righteousness of God (2 Corinthians 5:18-21 NIV).

In other words, Jesus took your sinning, your tendency and desire to sin, upon Himself as He hung on the cross. Everything that separated you from God the Father died in Jesus. Everything that prevented you from experiencing the power of God the Holy Spirit died in Jesus.

Jesus is your Savior, and He has the right to be your Lord. You have forgiveness, fellowship with the Father, and the indwelling of the Holy Spirit, who leads you into all truth.

Since you died with Jesus, you now have the power to die to yourself. Dying to yourself means rejecting the notion that everything in life revolves around you. By dying to yourself, you begin to see the gifts, goals, and needs of people under your authority.

Dying to yourself is difficult, sometimes even painful, because you are acknowledging that your old self no longer has the right to shape your identity and behavior.

When you die to your old self, you stop pursuing power and wealth as goals. You stop cutting corners. You quit trying to protect yourself. You stop lying and blaming other people.

By contrast, you begin to accept responsibility. You replace laziness with diligence, dishonesty with honesty, and cowardice with courage. You put other people's needs ahead of your own needs, and you lead them wisely.

Jesus stated:

> "Whoever wants to be my disciple must deny themselves and take up their cross daily and follow me. For whoever wants to save their life will lose it, but whoever loses their life for me will save it" (Luke 9:23-24 NIV).

God calls you to Servant Leadership, to a life of humility and self-denial, so that you bring glory to Him, while bringing grace and hope to others.

> Denying yourself is a challenge and at times it will feel painful. No one likes dying to self. It seems foreign or unnatural, so we resist it vigorously. Think about it this way: when you were born, life really did revolve around you. Your parents or other care givers recognized your needs, and they responded. If you were hungry, someone fed you. If you were tired, someone put you to bed. Someone bathed and clothed you. Someone watched over you when you were sick.

We all grow up with that idea, and we spend our lives developing an intense focus on self. Over time, mature persons understand that as an infant, we needed constant attention, but as an adult, we should outgrow this self-centeredness. The goal is maturity, whereby we learn to take care of ourselves and help others.

Once you understand that your old self died in Christ, you can enjoy a resurrected life. God has promised to raise His people to a new life, which means that your focus is on Him, where it belongs. It means looking out for the interests of your team and the others that you lead.

A resurrected life begins in the cemetery. The first step "downward" is to abandon selfishness and conceit, denying yourself daily, and acknowledging Jesus as your Savior, who died for you and rose again on your behalf.

Step Two:
View others as more important than yourself.
Philippians 2:3

The second step involves learning to value other people as more important than yourself. Remember:

Do nothing out of selfish ambition or vain conceit. Rather, in humility value others above yourselves, not looking to your own interests but each of you to the interests of the others (Philippians 2:3-4 NIV).

You must respect all people, no matter who they are or what they have. Racism is sinful. You should not look down on someone because he or she lacks education, money, possessions, or status.

Accordingly, you must understand that everyone is important; everyone has a purpose.

Think how different life would be if we believed that principle; we would see a transformation in the marketplace, in politics, in education, in families, and in the church.

Servant Leaders humble themselves and show respect to people *because* they know that all people are important to God.

Step Three:
Let your personal interests include the interest of others.
Philippians 2:4

Allow others to shape your interests as a servant leader. Obviously, you will think about your goals and desires, but effective Servant Leaders allow other people's interests to shape their thinking as well. I do not mean to suggest that you should become a doormat, nor should you lose your backbone. If God called you to lead people, then you should follow His direction. However, a Servant Leader should embrace other people's ideas and opinions and demonstrate grace and flexibility for the benefit of the individual and organization.

As we saw earlier, Jesus *emptied* Himself and *served* people from a heart of humility and compassion and God the Father *exalted* Him. Read Paul's words again:

> Therefore God exalted him to the highest place and gave him the name that is above every name, that at the name of Jesus every knee should bow, in heaven and on earth and under the earth, and every tongue acknowledge that Jesus Christ is Lord, to the glory of God the Father (Philippians 2:9-11 NIV).

Step Four:
A Servant Leader can rejoice that God exalts the humble.
Philippians 2:9-11

Servant Leaders rejoice when they humble themselves before the Lord. God is pleased with their willingness to serve others. God is pleased when they notice the quietest person in the room. God is pleased when they listen to others. God is pleased when they share the spotlight. *He will exalt the humble* in His time and in His way.

> Jesus' brother, the apostle James wrote, "Humble yourselves before the Lord, and he will lift you up" (James 4:10 NIV).

Peter echoed those words: "Humble yourselves, therefore, under God's mighty hand, that he may lift you up in due time" (1 Peter 5:6 NIV).

The path to success is a downward road, by which you move from self-indulgence and pride toward humility, submitting yourself to God and serving others.

Let's close with a statement by author C. William Pollard:

> Will the real leader please stand up? Not the president or the person with the most distinguished title or the longest tenure, but the role model. Not the highest paid person in the group but the risk taker. Not the person with the largest car or the biggest home, but the servant. Not the person who promotes himself or herself, but the promoter of others. Not the administrator, but the initiator. Not the taker, but the giver. Not the talker, but the listener.[89]

God has commissioned you to become a Servant Leader and, as such, you can influence the lives of men, women, and children across the nation and around the world. You can help to shape culture and leave a legacy that points people to the leadership of Jesus Christ, the greatest leader of all time.

The choice is yours. Will you accept the challenge?

Chapter 8 Review
"Embracing Humility"

- Servant Leaders understand that humility *energizes* them.

- Servant Leaders view humility as a strength, not a weakness.

- As the perfect model of Servant Leadership, Jesus offers to carry the burden and replace it with rest.

- In Matthew 11, Jesus says He is gentle and humble. This is the only time in the New Testament where Jesus describes Himself, that is, His heart; He *is* gentle and humble.

- HUMILITY means putting others first and downplaying one's personal desires; humility seeks to benefit everyone else.

  » Humility is thinking less of yourself and thinking more of others.

  » Humility says, "I understand that you have interests and so do I; nevertheless, I am willing to consider your interests above my own."

  » Humility chooses the "downward plunge" to elevate another person.

- Servant Leaders who emulate Jesus empty themselves of rank and privilege; they lay aside their preferences so that others can thrive.

- Embracing the "mind of Christ" is a life-long *process*. Servant Leaders typically progress in stages, developing habits that allow them to practice humility more consistently.

- There are four steps toward a "downward plunge" to greatness:

  » An effective Servant Leader must stop being selfish and conceited.

  » An effective Servant Leader must view others as more important than himself or herself.

  » An effective Servant Leader must let personal interests include the interest of others.

» An effective Servant Leader can rejoice that God exalts the humble.

+ An effective Servant Leader will embrace other people's ideas and opinions and demonstrate grace and flexibility for the benefit of the organization.

+ Servant Leaders rejoice when they humble themselves before the Lord.

  » They know that God is pleased with their willingness to serve the team.

  » They know that God is pleased when they notice the quietest person in the room.

  » They know that God is pleased when they listen to others.

  » They know that God is pleased when they share the spotlight.

+ Effective Servant Leaders know that the path to success is a downward road, by which they move from self-indulgence and pride toward humility, submitting themselves to God and serving others.

+ As a Servant Leader, you can help to shape culture and leave a legacy that points people to the leadership of Jesus Christ, the Greatest Leader of all time.

CHAPTER 9

A Seven Day Personal Application Guide to Servant Leadership

DAY ONE
CHAPTER 1: INTRODUCTION AND OVERVIEW

Take a few minutes to review your notes on the entire book. What grabbed your attention? Why?

_____

_____

_____

_____

_____

_____

_____

_____

What would God have you change in your personal leadership style so that you serve more like Jesus?

_____

_____

_____

_____

_____

_____

_____

_____

Based on the book, write out your personal definition of Servant Leadership.

_____

_____

_____

_____

_____

_____

_____

DAY TWO
CHAPTER 2: LEADERSHIP IS RISKY BUSINESS

Leadership is character-based. It is what ultimately drives what we do and why. Character is a true reflection of who we really are as human beings. It is what we need as leaders to meet the demands of reality. It is not a matter of outward technique, but of inner reality.

Turn to 2 Peter 1:5-8 and reflect on the qualities of character as they relate to you and your leadership. Write down the qualities that spoke to you.

_____

_____

_____

_____

_____

_____

_____

_____

_____

_____

_____

_____

DAY THREE
CHAPTER 3: FOLLOW THE LEADER

Evaluate yourself. Do you consider the needs of others above your own? (Y/N or both) Specify areas in life where you need to be less self-focused and write a short prayer asking for God's help to set your own desires aside.

_____

_____

_____

_____

_____

When Jesus left Heaven, He gave up everything to become a servant. Take some time to think deeply, reflectively. What hinders you from becoming a servant of others?

_____

_____

_____

_____

_____

What one thing will you begin to do TODAY to better serve your spouse?

_____

_____

_____

_____

_____

What one thing can you begin to do to better serve those under your leadership?

_____

_____

_____

DAY FOUR
CHAPTER 4: THE TEAM WITH A PURPOSE

Rate your leadership team according to the ten aspects of good teamwork.

_____

_____

_____

_____

_____

_____

_____

If you are the leader of a team, what is one thing you could do to make your team more effective?

_____

_____

_____

_____

_____

_____

_____

What actions steps will you take to accomplish this one thing?

_____

_____

_____

_____

_____

_____

_____

DAY FIVE
CHAPTER 5: BUILDING HEALTHY RELATIONSHIPS

Review the five truths of relationship for Servant Leaders. Where are you strong? Where are you weak? Explain.

_____

_____

_____

_____

_____

_____

_____

_____

Look again at the four building blocks of relationships. What is your strongest block? Why? What is your weakest block? What steps will you take to strengthen it?

_____

_____

_____

_____

_____

_____

_____

DAY SIX
CHAPTERS 6 & 7: UNDERSTANDING POWER, UNDERSTANDING AUTHORITY

1. Every leader has power to influence. As a leader how do you use your power to influence?

_____

_____

_____

_____

_____

2. Look again at the descriptions of a Power Leader and Servant Leader. Do you see yourself more as a Power Leader or a Servant Leader?

_____

_____

_____

_____

_____

3. What needs to change in your leadership to move you from Power Leadership to Servant Leadership?

_____

_____

_____

_____

_____

4. Picture yourself submitting your leadership to the authority of the Lordship of Christ and His interests. What would that look like? Describe the picture.

_____

_____

_____

DAY SEVEN
CHAPTER 8: EMBRACING HUMILITY

Read the following slowly. Reflect, meditate as you read, then pray it back to the Lord.

Lord of reality, make me real, not plastic, synthetic, pretend, phony, an actor playing out a part, a hypocrite.

I don't want to keep a prayer list but to pray, nor agonize to find your will but to obey what I already know, nor to argue theories of inspiration, but submit to your word.

I don't want to sing as if I mean it, I want to mean it.

I don't want to tell it like it is, but to be it like you want it.

I don't want to think another needs me, but I need him, else I'm not complete.

I don't want to tell others how to do it, but to do it. I don't have to be right always but to admit when I'm wrong.

I don't want to be a census-taker but an obstetrician; not an uninvolved person, a professional, but a friend.

I don't want to be insensitive, but to hurt where other people hurt, nor to say "I know how you feel" but to say, "God knows and I'll try if you'll be patient with me and meanwhile I'll be quiet."

I don't want to scorn the cliches of others but to mean everything I say, including this.

(A psalm of single-mindedness by Joe Bayly)

Selected Bibliography

Bass, B. M. *Bass & Stogdill's Handbook of Leadership*, 3rd ed. New York: Free Press, 1990.

Bennis, Warren and Burt Nanus. Leaders: The Strategies for Taking Charge. New York: Harper & Row, 1985.

Bennis, Warren and Robert Townsend. *Reinventing Leadership: Strategies to Empower the Organization*. New York: William Morrow and Company, 1985.

Borthwick, Paul. *Leading the Way*. NavPress Publishing Group, 1989. http://storage.cloversites.com/buildinggodlyfamilies/documents/Portrait%20of%20a%20Godly%20Leader.pdf.

Cloud, Henry. *Integrity*. New York: Harper Collins Publishing, 2006.

Cooperrider, David. Foreword to *The Power of Appreciative Inquiry: A Practical Guide to Positive Change*, by Diana Whitney and Amanda Trosten-Bloom, viii. San Francisco: Berrett-Koehler Publishers, Inc., 2010. Quoted by Andy Smith. "Peter Drucker on Strengths and Leadership." Coaching Leaders Ltd. https://coachingleaders.co.uk/peter-drucker-on-strengths-and-leadership/.

Cosgrove, Francis. "The Disciple Is a Servant." Discipleship Journal, no. 30 (1985): 35-38.

Day, David V. and John Antonakis. *The Nature of Leadership*, 2nd ed. California: SAGE Publications Ltd., 2012. http://www.sagepub.com/sites/default/files/upm-binaries/41161_1.pdf.

DePree, Max. *Leadership Is an Art*. New York: Doubleday, 1987.

DelHousaye, Darryl. *Servant Leadership*. Nashville: SBC Press, 2004.

Drucker, Peter. Management: *Tasks, Responsibilities, Practices*. New York: Harper Business, 1993.

Finzel, Hans. *The Top Ten Mistakes Leaders Make*. Wheaton: Victor Books, 1994.

Goldsmith, Marshall, John Baldoni, and Sarah McArthur, eds. *The AMA Handbook of Leadership*. Saranac Lake, NY: AMACOM, 2010. Quoted in "What is an Effective Leader?" American Management Association, 24 January 2019. https://www.amanet.org/articles/what-is-an-effective-leader-/.

Graham, Jill K. "Servant Leadership in Organizations: Inspirational and Moral." *Leadership Quarterly* 2, no. 2 (1991): 111.

Greenleaf, Robert K. *Servant Leadership*. New York: Paulist Press, 1977.

Hind, James F. *The Heart and Soul of Effective Management*. Wheaton: Victor Books, 1989.

Kouzes, James M. and Barry Z. Posner. *Credibility: How Leaders Gain It and Lose It, Why People Demand It*, 2nd ed. San Francisco: Jossey-Bass, 2 August 2011.

Levin, Marissa. "9 Leadership Behaviors That Lose Employee Trust and Respect." Inc., 9 February 2016. https://www.inc.com/marissa-levin/9-leadership-behaviors-that-lose-employee-trust-and-respect.html.

Lindsey, F. Duane. "The Call of the Servant in Isaiah 42:1-9." Bibliothecra Sacra 139, no. 14 (January - March 1982): 28.

Llopis, Glen. "6 Ways Effective Listening Can Make You a Better Leader." Forbes: Leadership Strategy, May 2013. https://www.forbes.com/sites/glennllopis/2013/05/20/6-effective-ways-listening-can-make-you-a-better-leader/#265270ab1756.

Means, James. Leadership in Christian Ministry. Grand Rapids: Baker Book House, 1989.

Miller, Mark. The Heart of Leadership: Becoming a Leader People Want to Follow. Oakland, CA: Berrett-Koehler Publishers, 2011.

Miller, Mark. The Heart of Leadership Field Guide. Tucker, GA: CFA Properties and InterGREAT Leadership, 2020.

Nichols, Ralph G. and Leonard A. Stevens. "Listening to People." Harvard Business Review, September 1957. https://hbr.org/1957/09/listening-to-people.

Nouwen, Henri J. M. In the Name of Jesus: Reflections on Christian Leadership. Chestnut Ridge, NY: Crossroad, 1992. Quoted in "The Leading Edge, A Study Series to Develop Spiritual Leadership for the Global Marketplace." Christian Businessmen's Connection, Inc., chap 5. https://www.cbmc.com/files/leading-edge/leadingedge5.pdf.

Parker, Glenn M. Team Players and Teamwork: New Strategies for Developing Successful Collaboration. Hoboken, NY: Jossey-Bass, February 2008. https://archive.org/details/teamplayersteam-w00park_1/mode/2up?q=ability+of+team+members+to+listen+to+each+other.

Pollard, C. William. "The Leader Who Serves." in Leader of the Future, edited by Francis Hesselbein, Marshall Goldsmith, and Richard Beckhard, 242. San Francisco: Jossey Bass Publishers, 1996.

Porath, Christine. "Half of Employees Don't Feel Respected by Their Bosses." Harvard Business Review, 19 November 2014. https://hbr.org/2014/11/half-of-employees-dont-feel-respected-by-their-bosses.

Posner, James M. and Barry Z. Credibility: How Leaders Gain and Lose It, Why People Demand It. San Francisco: Jossey-Bass Publishers, 1983.

Richards, Lawrence O. and Clyde Hoeldtke. *A Theology of Church Leadership*. Grand Rapids: Zondervan Corporation, 1980.

Rush, Myron. *The New Leader*. Wheaton: Victor Books, 1987.

Sanders, J. Oswald. *Servant Leadership: Principles of Excellence for Every Believer*. Chicago: Moody Publishers, 2017.

Sanders, J. Oswald. *Spiritual Leadership*. Chicago: Moody Press, 1967.

Stetzer, Ed. "Defining Leadership: What Is It and Why Does It Matter in Church?" *Christianity Today*, December 2019. https://www.christianitytoday.com/edstetzer/2019/september/defining-leadership-christian-serving-god-empower-people.html.

Stott, John R.W. *The Gospel and the End of Time: The Message of 1 & 2 Thessalonians*. Downers Grove, IL: InterVarsity Press, 1991. https://www.insight.org/resources/daily-devotional/individual/his-only-priority.

Swindoll, Charles. *Majestic Meekness*. Wheaton, IL: Crossway, 2012. https://www.crossway.org/tracts/majestic-meekness-3143/.

Additional Resources

Fred Campbell, *How a Church can Develop a Leadership Culture*

Fred Campbell, Servant Leadership Workshop – Conducted in a local church setting.

Fred Campbell, *Leadership Nuggets from the Greatest Servant of All. Leadership Insights from the Gospel of Mark.* An excellent leadership devotional.

To order all resources, write to fred@livinggraceministries.com

Endnotes

[1]History.com Editors, "Alexander the Great," History.com, A & E Television Networks, LLC., updated 21 February 2020, accessed 11June 2020, https://www.history.com/topics/ancient-history/alexander-the-great.

[2]Leonid Alexseyevich Nikiforov, "Peter I, Emperor of Russia," Encyclopedia Britannica, Encyclopedia Britannica, Inc., 5 June 2020, accessed 11 June 2020, https://www.britannica.com/biography/Peter-the-Great.

[3]Denise Chow, "5 Influential Leaders Who Transformed the World," LiveScience, Future US, Inc., 6 December 2013, accessed 2 September 2020, https://www.livescience.com/41742-influential-leaders-who-transformed-the-world.html.

[4]David V. Day and John Antonakis, *The Nature of Leadership, 2nd ed.* (California: SAGE Publications Ltd., 2012), chap. 1, accessed 10 June 2020, http://www.sagepub.com/sites/default/files/upm-binaries/41161_1.pdf.

[5]Ibid.

[6]Ibid.

[7]Ibid.

[8]Ibid.

[9]Ibid.

[10]Ibid.

[11]Ibid.

[12]Braden Becker, "The 8 Most Common Leadership Styles & How to Find Your Own," Marketing (blog), Hubspot, Inc., 7 February 2020, updated 11 February 2020, accessed 11 June 2020, https://blog.hubspot.com/marketing/leadership-styles.

[13]Stephen Ornes, "Flipping Icebergs: Capsizing icebergs may release energy as a bomb," ScienceNewsforStudents, Society for Science & the Public, 3 April 2012, accessed 15 June 2020, https://www.sciencenewsforstudents.org/article/flipping-icebergs.

[14]"Just the Facts," Canadian Geographic Exploration and Discovery Magazine CG In-Depth: Icebergs, Canadian Geographic Enterprises, 31 March 2006, accessed 15 June 2020, https://web.archive.org/web/20060331032737/https://www.canadiangeographic.ca/magazine/MA06/indepth/justthefacts.asp.

[15]Ibid.

[16]Jim Rohn, "Rohn: 6 Essential Traits of Good Character." Success (online), 9 October 2016, accessed 15 June 2020, https://www.success.com/rohn-6-essential-traits-of-good-character/.

[17]James M. Kouzes and Barry Z. Posner, Credibility: How Leaders Gain It and Lose It, Why People Demand It, 2nd ed. (San Francisco: Jossey-Bass, 2 August 2011).

[18]"Kouzes and Posner Leadership Participation Inventory Model in Transformational Leadership," StudiousGuy.com, accessed 15 June 2020, https://studiousguy.com/kouzes-and-posner-leadership-participation-inventory-model-in-transformational-leadership/.

[19]Max DePree, Leadership Is an Art (New York: Doubleday, 1987), xxii, Coursehero.com, accessed 15 June 2020, https://www.coursehero.com/file/20801445/Leadership-is-an-Art/.

[20]Ibid, 10.

[21]Roger Carr, "70/30 Rule for Small Group Leaders," Smallgroupinternational.com (blog), accessed 15 June 2020, https://www.smallgroupinternational.com/70-30-rule-small-group-leaders/.

[22]Joe Ioracchi, "4 Reasons Humility is a Cardinal Virtue in Servant Leadership," Serveleadnow.com (blog), Cairnway, LLC., accessed 15 June 2020, https://serveleadnow.com/blog-4-reasons-humility/.

[23]James F. Hind, The Heart and Soul of Effective Management (Wheaton: Victor Books, 1989), 55.

[24]Darryl DelHousaye, Servant Leadership (Nashville: SBC Press, 2004), 42.

[25]Trevin Wax, "Revising Oswald Sanders' 'Spiritual Leadership,'" Thegospelcoalition.org (blog), The Gospel Coalition, 27 August 2014, accessed 15 June 2020, https://www.thegospelcoalition.org/blogs/trevin-wax/revisiting-oswald-sanders-spiritual-leadership/.

[26]Ibid.

[27]J. Oswald Sanders, Servant Leadership: Principles of Excellence for Every Believer (Chicago: Moody Publishers, 2017), 18.

[28]Warren Bennis and Burt Nanus, Leaders: The Strategies for Taking Charge (New York: Harper & Row, 1985), 4.

[29]Hans Finzel, The Top Ten Mistakes Leaders Make (Wheaton: Victor Books, 1994), 13.

[30]Henry Cloud, Integrity (New York: Harper Collins Publishing, 2006), 24.

[31]Biography.com Editors, "Edward J. Smith Biography," Biography.com, A&E Television Networks, LLC., 2 April 2014, updated 2 August 2019, accessed 12 June 2020, https://www.biography.com/historical-figure/edward-j-smith.

[32]Ibid.

[33]Ibid.

[34]Ibid.

[35]Radio Times Team, "Titanic: myths sunk! Historian Tim Maltin sets the record straight about the sinking of the Titanic," Radiotimes.com, Immediate Media Company Ltd., 4 October 2012, accessed 12 June 2020, https://www.radiotimes.com/news/2012-04-10/titanic-myths-sunk/.

36   Ibid.

37   Ibid.

[38]Ibid.

[39]Ibid.

[40]J. Oswald Sanders, Spiritual Leadership (Chicago: Moody Press, 1967), 21.

[41]Hans Finzel, The Top Ten Mistakes Leaders Make (Wheaton: Victor Books, 1994), 13, 17-18.

[42]Lawrence O. Richards and Clyde Hoeldtke, A Theology of Church Leadership (Grand Rapids: Zondervan Corporation, 1980), 103-104.

[43]Phil Quigley, "Leadership: What Others are Saying" Servant Leadership Library, Bivocational and Small Church Leadership Network, accessed 16 July 2020, https://bscln.net/resources/servant-leadership-library/what-others-are-saying-sl18/.

[44]James M. and Barry Z. Posner, Credibility: How Leaders Gain and Lose It, Why People Demand It (San Francisco: Jossey-Bass Publishers, 1983), 1.

[45]Max DePree, Leadership Is an Art (New York: Dell Trade Paperback,1989), 3.

[46]Darryl DeHousaye, "The Essence of Servant Leadership" (DMin diss., Western Conservative Baptist Seminary, 1995), 15-16.

[47]Myron Rush, The New Leader (Wheaton: Victor Books, 1987), 87.

[48]F. Duane Lindsey, "The Call of the Servant in Isaiah 42:1-9," Bibliothecra Sacra 139, no. 14 (January- March 1982): 28.

[49]Robert K. Greenleaf, Servant Leadership (New York: Paulist Press, 1977), 7, 10.

[50]Ibid.

[51]Francis Cosgrove, "The Disciple Is a Servant," Discipleship Journal, no. 30 (1985): 35-38.

[52]C. William Pollard, "The Leader Who Serves," in Leader of the Future, eds. Francis Hesselbein, Marshall Goldsmith, and Richard Beckhard (San Francisco: Jossey Bass Publishers, 1996), 242.

[53]Jill K. Graham, "Servant Leadership in Organizations: Inspirational and Moral," Leadership Quarterly 2, no. 2 (1991): 111.

[54]James Means, Leadership in Christian Ministry (Grand Rapids: Baker Book House, 1989), 48.

[55]John Richard Love, "A Documentary Evaluation of the Project Cathedral Hypothesis Regarding Leadership" (DMin diss., Dallas Theological Seminary, 1992), ii.

[56]Dr. Howard Hendricks, Leadership Course, Dallas Theological Seminary, 1969.

[57]Henri J. M. Nouwen, In the Name of Jesus: Reflections on Christian Leadership (Chestnut Ridge, NY: Crossroad, 1992), quoted in "The Leading Edge, A Study Series to Develop Spiritual Leadership for the Global Marketplace," Christian Business Men's Connection, Inc., chap 5, accessed 16 June 2020, https://www.cbmc.com/files/leadingedge/leadingedge5.pdf.

[58]Charles Swindoll, Majestic Meekness (Wheaton, IL: Crossway, 2012), 1, accessed 17 July 2020, https://www.crossway.org/tracts/majestic-meekness-3143/.

[59]Gordon Fee, quoted in "Who is Jesus (Part 1): The Humility of Christ Philippians 2:5-7," Hickory Grove Advent Christian Church (blog), accessed 17 July 2020, https://grovenc.church/portfolio/who-is-jesus-part-1-the-humility-of-christ-philippians-25-7/.

[60]"What is a bondservant? How are bondservants viewed in the Bible?" Compelling Truth (online), Got Questions Ministries, accessed 17 June 2020, https://www.compellingtruth.org/bondservant.html.

[61]Thomas L. McDonald, "Understanding the Washing of the Feet," God and the Machine (blog), Patheos, published 1 April 2015, accessed 17 June 2020, https://www.patheos.com/blogs/godandthemachine/2015/04/washing-of-the-feet/.

[62]Katy Devereaux, "Angie Garber Lived a Life of Love." Grace Connect, Brethren Missionary Herald Company, 1 January 2007, accessed 17 June 2020, https://graceconnect.us/angie-garber-lived-a-life-of-love/.

[63]John Bartlett, Bartlett's Familiar Quotations, 17th ed., ed. Justin Kaplan (Boston: Little, Brown, and Company, 2002), 320:18.

[64]Ralph G. Nichols and Leonard A. Stevens, "Listening to People," Harvard Business Review (online archive), September 1957, accessed 24 June 2020, https://hbr.org/1957/09/listening-to-people.

[65]Rebecca Lake, "Listening Statistics: 23 Facts You Need to Hear" Best Personal Finance Podcasts, CreditDonkey, 17 September 2015, accessed 24 June 2020, https://www.creditdonkey.com/listening-statistics.html.

[66]Glen Llopis, "6 Ways Effective Listening Can Make You a Better Leader," Forbes: Leadership Strategy, 20 May 2013, accessed 24 June 2020, https://www.forbes.com/sites/glennllopis/2013/05/20/6-effective-ways-listening-can-make-you-a-better-leader/#265270ab1756.

[67]"Chicago Bulls Overview," Champsorchumps.us, accessed 24 June 2020, https://champsorchumps.us/team/nba/chicago-bulls.

[68]Peter Drucker, quoted by David Cooperrider, foreword to The Power of Appreciative Inquiry: A Practical Guide to Positive Change, by Diana Whitney and Amanda Trosten-Bloom (San Francisco: Berrett-Koehler Publishers, Inc., 2010), viii, quoted by Andy Smith, "Peter Drucker on Strengths and Leadership," Coaching Leaders Ltd., accessed 24 June 2020, https://coachingleaders.co.uk/peter-drucker-on-strengths-and-leadership/.

[69]Glenn M. Parker, Team Players and Teamwork: New Strategies for Developing Successful Collaboration (Hoboken, NY: Jossey-Bass, February 2008), 32, accessed 14 July 2020, https://archive.org/details/teamplayersteamw00park_1/mode/2up?q=ability+of+team+members+to+listen+to+each+other.

[70]J. Oswald Sanders, Spiritual Leadership, quoted in Ken Weliever. "Great Verses of the Bible: Acts 20:28," ThePreachersWord, 9 May 2018, accessed 13 July 2020, https://thepreachersword.com/2018/05/09/great-verses-of-the-bible-acts-2028/.

[71]Ibid.[72]John D. Rockefeller, BrainyQuote, accessed 26 June 2020, https://www.brainyquote.com/search_results?q=rockefeller+ability+to+deal+with+people.

[73]Theodore Roosevelt, BrainyQuote, accessed 26 June 2020, https://www.brainyquote.com/search_results?q=+ingredient%2C+the+Paramount%27s+skill%2C+what%27s+the+ability+.

[74]Marshall Goldsmith, John Baldoni, and Sarah McArthur, eds., The AMA Handbook of Leadership, (AMACOM, 2010), quoted in "What is an Effective Leader?" American Management Association (online), 24 January 2019, accessed 26 June 2020, https://www.amanet.org/articles/what-is-an-effective-leader-/.

[75]Lee Iacocca, BrainyQuote, accessed 26 June 2020, https://s3.amazonaws.com/davidhmckinley/outline/2002/LifeFOCUS/020925_notes.pdf.

[76]National Soft Skills Association, "The Real Skills Gap," Research and Publications, National Soft Skills Association, 8 April 2016, accessed 20 July 2020, https://www.nationalsoftskills.org/the-real-skills-gap/.

[77]John R.W. Stott, *The Gospel and the End of Time: The Message of 1 & 2 Thessalonians* (Downers Grove, IL: InterVarsity Press, 1991), 47, accessed 26 June 2020, https://www.insight.org/resources/daily-devotional/individual/his-only-priority.

[78]Marissa Levin, "9 Leadership Behaviors That Lose Employee Trust and Respect," Inc., 9 February 2016, accessed 29 June 2020, https://www.inc.com/marissa-levin/9-leadership-behaviors-that-lose-employee-trust-and-respect.html.

[79]Christine Porath, "Half of Employees Don't Feel Respected by Their Bosses," Harvard Business Review,19 November 2014, accessed 29 June 2020, https://hbr.org/2014/11/half-of-employees-dont-feel-respected-by-their-bosses.

[80]Paul Borthwick, Leading the Way (NavPress Publishing Group, 1989), 177-178, accessed 29 June 2020, http://storage.cloversites.com/buildinggodlyfamilies/documents/Portrait%20of%20a%20Godly%20Leader.pdf.

[81]Nouwen, 58-60.

[82]Nouwen, 44-45.

[83]Warren Bennis and Robert Townsend, Reinventing Leadership: Strategies to Empower the Organization (New York: William Morrow and Company, 1985), 43.

[84]James Orr, M.A, D.D., ed., "Entry for INTEGRITY," International Standard Bible Encyclopedia, 1915, Bible Study Tools, https://www.biblestudytools.com/encyclopedias/isbe/integrity.html.

[85]Peter Drucker, Management: Tasks, Responsibilities, Practices

(New York: Harper Business, April 14, 1993 reprint edition), 301.

[86]B. M. Bass, Bass & Stogdill's Handbook of Leadership, 3rd ed. (New York: Free Press, 1990), 233- 247.

[87]Richards, 318-319.

[88]Ed Stetzer, "Defining Leadership: What Is It and Why Does It Matter in Church?" Christianity Today, 6 December 2019, accessed 6 July 6, 2020, https://www.christianitytoday.com/edstetzer/2019/september/defining-leadership-christian-serving-god-empower-people.html.

[89]C. William Pollard, "A Leader Who Serves," C. William Pollard Papers, (Seattle Pacific University Library: 22 October 1997), 5, accessed 8 July 2020, https://digitalcommons.spu.edu/pollard_papers/115.

About the Author

Servant leadership is a passion for Fred Campbell. He served for 23 years as the founding senior pastor of Faith Bible Church in the Dallas metroplex. During that time, he established a solid leadership team of elders, deacons, pastoral staff, and ministry leaders. Fred was also a senior faculty member of PromiseKeepers, working with other leaders to teach men's educational seminars. In September 1998, he became the pastor of Grace Church of Ovilla, a church he also helped to start. Once again, Fred established a strong leadership team for the church. He retired from Grace Church in October 2015, to serve in a more active role with Living Grace Ministries.

Fred has worked with Global Missions Fellowship in evangelistic/church planting campaigns in Brazil and Venezuela. He has taught leadership conferences in 29 countries and 15 states.

LIVING GRACE MINISTRIES

Since 1998, Living Grace Ministries, under the leadership of Dr. Fred C. Campbell, has provided The Authentic Servant Leadership Workshop for pastors and their leadership teams. Its focus is to help church leaders develop servant leaders by following the model of the greatest leader of all time, Jesus Christ. Other leaders have stood out in history, but only One was perfect. The Authentic Servant Leadership Workshop captures the essence of Jesus' leadership style through teaching and interactive discussion by the participants.

Made in the USA
Columbia, SC
31 July 2021